IN DEFIANCE
OUR STORIES

Short Fiction by Dalit Writers

Translated by

Malini Seshadri & V Ramakrishnan

Vitasta
LET KNOWLEDGE SPREAD

TAMILNADU TEXTBOOK AND EDUCATIONAL SERVICES CORPORATION
LEARN THOROUGHLY

Published by
Renu Kaul Verma
Vitasta Publishing Pvt Ltd
2/15, Ansari Road, Daryaganj
New Delhi - 110 002
info@vitastapublishing.com

ISBN 978-93-90961-44-3

English translation

First Edition 2022
MRP ₹ 450

The contents of this book do not reflect the views of the publisher, editors and the translators. The Tamil Nadu Textbook and Educational Services Corporation is not responsible for the views expressed here.

This is a work of fiction and all characters and incidents described in this book are the product of the authors' imagination. Any resemblance to actual persons, living or dead, is entirely coincidental.

Cover & Layout by Somesh Kumar Mishra
Printed by Chaman Enterprises, Delhi

TRANSLATION INITIATIVE OF THE TAMIL NADU TEXTBOOK AND EDUCATIONAL SERVICES CORPORATION

This is an initiative of the Tamil Nadu Textbook and Educational Services Corporation (TNTB & ESC) under the aegis of GO. Ms. No. 207, SE(TRB) Dept., Dated 22.09.2017, action plan 6, to identify and translate into English, Tamil literary works, that they might enhance the reach of Tamil antiquity, tradition and contemporaneity and enrich world literature to also translate significant literary voices for other languages into Tamil. Both ventures are to be undertaken as either an Independent or Joint publications with collaborating publishers.

Members, Academic Advising Committee (Translation)

Dr. R. Balakrishnan, IAS, Researcher and Writer
Thiru. S. Ramakrishnan, Writer
Thiru. S. Madasamy, Educationist

Project Execution Team

Thiru. Dindigul I. Leoni, Chairperson, TNTB & ESC
Dr. D. Manikandan IAS, Managing Director, TNTB & ESC
Dr. Nagaraja Murugan, Member Secretary, TNTB & ESC
Thiru. R. Dhayalan, Financial Advisor, TNTB & ESC
Dr. T. S. Saravanan, Deputy Director (Translations), TNTB & ESC
Thiru. K. Subramani, Deputy Director (Publications), TNTB & ESC
Thiru. M. Appanasamy, Consultant, TNTB & ESC
Tmt. Mini Krishnan, Co-ordinating Editor, TNTB & ESC

CONTENTS

Introduction *vii*

Translator's Note *xi*

Translator's Note *xv*

Wetness
Cho Dharuman 1

Ponnammai
Kovedha Swaminathan 10

Street Theatre
V Venkatachalam 21

Bhogi Has Come And Gone
Gowthama Sannah 32

For A Handful Of Rice
Abimani 40

A Rare Flower
P Sivakami 48

The Government School
Imayam 70

The Sweetest Fruit
Theynmozhi 87

Annaachi
Bama 105

The Unique Letter
Ravikumar 114

Bro 'T'
Pratibha Jeyachandran 121

Yet Another Rainy Season
Pablo Arivukkuyil 139

Eardrum
Azhagiya Periyavan 157

Palla Street
Vizhi Pa Idhayavendhan 169

Contributors *183*

About the Translators *189*

INTRODUCTION

I am delighted that this collection which I put together for the Sahitya Akademi some years ago is now being published by Vitasta Publihsing Pvt Ltd & the Tamil Nadu Textbook Corporation. Most of them are from my original plan. A few are from other collections, and yet others completely fresh selections and translations.

Starting from the 1980s, Dalit stories have been influencing the course of Tamil literature. The growth of Dalit writing has been such that the mere handful of such writers in the 1980s has swelled into more than a hundred on current count. Yet the number of women among them is still low. This reflects the reality that literacy levels among Dalit women remain poor.

Not only have the numbers of Dalit authors risen over the decades, but the ambit of the themes they tackle has also widened. Understanding that literature could serve as a tool for social activism, Dalit writers skilfully used the short story as semi-fictionalized records to creatively share the experiences of caste and their own responses to it. They have also come to the fore in writing essays and treatises on societal issues as seen from a Dalit perspective, exploring traditional songs and lore handed down through the oral tradition, recording authentic Dalit history, carrying out research studies on the entrenched caste paradigms, and voicing the Dalit population's economic concerns, about land ownership, housing and the basic necessities of life. Alongside this, active efforts are under way to translate into Tamil many Dalit writings in other Indian languages.

However, given the fact that it is the poets, novelists and short story writers who are the most visible face of Tamil literature, the same is true for Tamil Dalit writing as well.

In general, it had been assumed that 'Dalit writing' was the output exclusively of those who had been born Dalit. This was something that was arrived at after much discussion and accepted as fact by everyone. I too was one among those who subscribed to this view.

Even the women writers who championed the need for 33 percent reservation for women did not demand a quota for Dalit women from among this percentage. From this one could assume a kind of equivalence in outlook. Women writers championing a greater role for women is mirrored by Dalit writers demanding social justice.

Although many may find it unpalatable to accept this situation, it has become clear that there is a growing awareness amongst Dalits of their rights. Those who had assumed that they would be intimidated by the hurdles in their path have begun to alter their own perspectives.

Up till recently, Tamil writers had mainly portrayed Dalits only as servants, minions or ignorant simpletons mired in poverty. Even in Marxist writings, Dalits were subsumed under the general umbrella of the 'poor'. In this scenario, it was Dalit writing that first depicted Dalits as respectable protagonists in their stories, men and women with their own valid opinions and views. It gave them an identity as those who had been unjustly relegated to a backward status in society, and united them as a community of like-minded people. This is indeed a stupendous achievement.

Also, by moving beyond the hitherto clichéd depiction of village life with its *katta panchayats* as the arbiters of justice, and casting the spotlight on *cheri* life instead, these writers showed that there are villages within villages, each with their distinctive aesthetics. One could say that it is only through Dalit writing that Tamil readers were introduced to authentic village life.

Dalit literature, pioneered by Poomani, P Sivakami, and Bama, and taken forward by Imayam, Pratibha Jeyachandran, Vizhi. Pa. Idhayavendan, Kovedha Swaminathan, Abimaani, Madivannan, Anbaadhavan, Sridhara Ganesan, Azhagiya Periyavan and Pallo Arivukuyil has been further strengthened by the advent of newer writers such as Amirtham Surya, V Venkatachalam, Bhavani, Kudiarasan and Gowthama Sannah.

Today no anthology of Tamil fiction is complete without contributions from Dalit writers and the publication of anthologies of Tamil Dalit writing by multinational publishers in the first decade of this century was a sign that Tamil literary output today has been impacted and altered forever by the Dalit sensibility.

P. Sivakami
Writer and Activist

TRANSLATOR'S NOTE

Malini Seshadri

I have translated nine of the stories in this collection. These stories are works of fiction. Yet they could well be seen as docu-dramas. Between the writer and the protagonist is an intimacy that can come only from breathing the same air. Indeed, I view this as the hallmark of 'Dalit writing', a reporting of life's daily dramas big and small in real time, which lends a note of immediacy, of urgency, to the events as they unfold.

I therefore see it as an added responsibility to try to mirror this intimacy as well as this immediacy, while navigating the cross currents of moving the text from its native language to an alien one.

I have had a fair amount of experience in translating works by Tamil Dalit writers; which is not to say that the task gets simpler. Each work has its own special attributes and challenges. This collection is no different.

Sometimes the equivalent falls into place easily with a click. For instance, I could celebrate when "those years slipped by like a slippery palm fruit sliding down the throat." But those 'aha' moments are few. Much of the work involves phrasing and rephrasing, tweaking and embellishing, in an attempt to retain the flavour of the original phrasing while also retaining the emotional content. Like Heisenberg's Principle of Uncertainty, a translator's attempt at achieving total accuracy of one variable causes a degree of uncertainty in another variable. This see-saw cannot often be exactly balanced.

Not only does the translator need to address language and style issues so that the reader experiences a good 'flow', but also has to stay within the cultural milieu of the original. I find that the latter is often the greater challenge. For instance, many of these stories are set within the intricate hierarchical caste structure of a village, which could well be an impenetrable maze for the uninformed reader. There are rules of engagement, lines in the sand that cannot be crossed without incurring dire consequences. These are mind-boggling to the uninitiated person, but are absorbed along with the mother's milk by the locals. A route map through the maze had to be indicated, either with strategically placed phrases in the text or with an explanatory note.

The dominant themes are deprivation, destitution and despotism. Emotions range from anger to sorrow, from hope to despair. But irony, even humour, are often not far under the surface. Each story has its unique signature touches. Ammaasi finds out that one word, one form of address, is the difference between subservience and impertinence. Ponnu the retired koothu artiste tugs at the reader's heartstrings, while the children celebrating Bhogi elicit a smile tinged with sorrow. What have snakes got to do with magic and mystique? What is the significance of a special mountainside flower? How are drums made in the village and what is a drummer's life? How did Lazarus rise from the dead yet again? I found answers to these and many more riddles among these pages.

I am grateful to Mini Krishnan for her suggestions and inputs which have enhanced the quality of the translations.

I hope readers will find many hidden rewards here as well. I am glad that the Tamil Nadu Textbook Corporation (TNTB) identified this collection for their translation project.

TRANSLATOR'S NOTE

V Ramakrishnan

I have translated five of the stories in this collection. I sincerely hope that in translating the lives in these stories for a global audience, I have done some justice to the original stories in Tamil. These stories convey more than what their words contain: be it the tale of revenge, or the story of an estranged woman, or the slice-of-life narratives from the ordinary lives of common people, these stories stand beyond easy categorisation and portray events that often go unperceived.

The task of translation involves many compromises. In addition to the primary objective of rendering the text in another language, translation is burdened with the responsibility of closely reflecting the cultural setting of the source. In culturally loaded contexts like those of the stories in this anthology, every element, ranging from the dialect spoken by the characters to their food and lifestyle, needs to be given due thought before it is translated. Considering the difference between Tamil and English cultures, making these choices is often challenging, and the outcome may sometimes feel inadequate. I have attempted to straddle the twin objectives of capturing the cultural context of the source and making the narrative flow naturally in English. I must admit that compromises had to be made on both sides to accomplish it.

The 'compromise' mentioned above can be demonstrated with how relationships have been handled in one of the stories. The Tamil word "maama", sripped of context, can simply be translated as "uncle". But, in this story, when the female protagonist talks about her "maama", she refers to her fiancé (who happens to be her cousin). In Tamil culture, it is common for women to call their spouses "maama". At the same time, when she talks about her fiancé's "maama", she refers to his uncle (i.e., her own father). Now, translating "maama" becomes problematic. Given the context, I made a conscious decision to refer to her fiancé as "maama" and to refer to her father as "his uncle". To make matters worse, the protagonist's father's younger brother also appears in the story. Since the English equivalent for the relationship—uncle—would create more confusion, I have retained the Tamil word "chithappa" in the story for clarity.

Similarly, some conscious word choices have been made even if the output doesn't sound natural in English. For example, to truly reflect a cultural setting where school children do not refer to their teachers by name, I have made a deliberate choice to retain the local usage of "teacher" or "master". So, when a student appears at the doorstep of the Headmaster saying, "Teacher asked me to meet you, sir", it is a compromise made on what sounds natural in English.

On the other hand, where the cultural context of the

source does not have much impact on the story, I have also chosen to go by proper English usages that sound natural. When a lady proudly repeats that she is a "roshakkaari", though it is hard to come up with a perfect equivalent for the Tamil word, I have chosen an expression closest in meaning ("I have dignity, you know… I'm dignified") for it to sound natural in English.

I would like to thank my professor, Dr. R. Azhagarasan, whose sharp eye for nuances in translation has helped me appreciate the subtleties of the craft. Translating these stories has been a delightful challenge and a journey full of surprising discoveries, for we seldom pay close attention to things close to us. In that sense, this exercise has opened my eyes to some intricacies in Tamil and English, both linguistic and cultural. I am grateful to Mrs. Mini Krishnan who offered me very helpful guidance with these translations.

I am happy that these stories are being brought to a wider readership through the translation project of the Tamil Nadu Textbook Corporation (TNTB).

WETNESS

CHO DHARUMAN

Even after a full three days the rain showed no signs of stopping. It came down in drizzles and flurries, and the overcast sky was roiling and heaving with endless banks of clouds. The sun had not shown his face even once. Maybe now and then the hint of a pause in the downpour…the false promise of sunlight breaking through…but then again a spell of rain. As Kokku Thatha was fond of remarking, '*Thaayili*! What a rain! Brings ruin when it comes, leaves ruin when it goes. Like a daughter-in-law's tears for her dead mother-in-law, this rain…dreadful…that's what it is…'

Yes, this was one such rain. All the people of the street huddled indoors. All work was at a standstill.

Thangammal sat on the floor with her legs stretched out. On her lap she had spread a white saree, and was busy picking out the lice that were crawling across it. She poked at them, and snapped them to death between her teeth and

---

Translated by Malini Seshadri
Original Source: *'Eeram'*, Cho Dharumanin Kathaikal, 2001
English Translation: *The Oxford India Anthology of Tamil Dalit Writing* edited by Ravikumar & R. Azhagarasan (OUP, 2012)

spat them out. Once again she picked up the close-toothed comb and passed it through her hair to dislodge more lice. Sivakami sat on the front step staring intently at the rain. She watched as the raindrops falling on the waterlogged courtyard formed their own miniature fountains that dissolved and reappeared endlessly.

'*Amma*, when will this accursed rain stop?'

'Only when both you and I are dead.'

Her mother's ill-tempered reply made Sivakami retreat into silence once more. For a while neither of them spoke. Except for the steady sound of the still-falling rain, there was utter silence.

'Why do you have to be so irritable, *Ma*, as if you had just bitten into a dry chilli?'

'What do you expect, then? When will it rain, when will it stop raining…am I the *josiakarar* Keezhnaattukurichi Iyer to predict all this?

'I am not asking for any *josyam*. What's for dinner?'

'Go and scrape up a potful of wet mud…that will be the dinner for the two of us.'

Again Sivakami was intensely irritated by her mother's response. But she knew very well what to expect next if she were to retort. So she restrained herself and did not speak. Except for the sound of the raindrops, there was an empty silence. Sivakami raised her eyes and looked at her mother.

'At least you could go to the Company and ask for ten rupees as advance,' she said.

'Hah, yes, the Company! You think it is your Appa's Company and so they will gladly hand over whatever we ask? That loan I took to buy your *paavaadais*...that hasn't been returned yet. Where's the question of advance now?'

'If Appa had owned a company and lived comfortably, why would I be struggling at your hands like this now? The lucky man departed this world only because he did not want to see this wretched sight. Why are you dragging his name into this now?'

'*Adiye*, are you going to shut up this minute or do you want me to give you a good thrashing with the broom?'

'All this doesn't bother you. You're able to clench your teeth and bear the hunger and live only on water for eight days. I am so hungry....'

'Hungry, are you? Come here, come and bite off my flesh...chew and eat.'

Sivakami rose, muttering, from the doorstep. She looked for and picked up a torn and tattered piece of sacking and a bundle of old clothes, went up the steps and lay down. The wetness of the floor, the dampness of the old sack, and the growling hunger in her belly seemed to tug at her tired eyelids. Soon she was asleep.

Thangammal shook out the cloth on her lap, drew up her knees and reached for the fine-toothed comb that was tucked next to her big toe. She looked up and saw that Sivakami was deep in sleep.

Thangammal gazed unblinkingly at her daughter for a long while. The tears welled up in her eyes. She sobbed soundlessly. Her teeth bit down hard on her lower lip as she wept. In front of her was the plank that had been used as a pasting surface, and on top of it lay the wooden sealing stick, a stack of cards from the Company, and an old tin containing a mixture of yam flour and zinc yet to be boiled to make a paste. At the corner of the *thinnai* stood the paste pot, with its short-handled ladle still stuck in it. At the edges of the pot the paste had dried into big, hard lumps. Thangammal wiped her eyes with the edge of her saree. Her face mirrored the torment in her mind.

'What a wretched job! A killer of a job...better to die than to live with a job like this. If it's a coolie job in the fields they give you one day's work and then for nine days there is nothing. But even that seems better than this matchbox factory job. No sun, the boxes are still wet...so the factory is shut. No chloride...shut for ten days. Labels haven't arrived...so shut. Then they shut for ten days with no explanation at all...and then what do they say? They say the stocks haven't moved. They claim they are thinking of making a change in the size....With all this, finally only ten days of work in the month. During *Aipasi* and *Karthigai*, virtually no work at all...during summer slogging day and night. All those thousands like us who are depending on this kind of job for their survival...a constant struggle to find enough to feed the belly and cover the body...waiting for the release of death...what sort of wretched life is this? One must live a decent existence like a normal human being... otherwise far better to die than lead this dog's life....'

Sivakami turned over restlessly and curled up in her sleep. Thangammal looked at her daughter and wept uncontrollably. She stuffed the edge of her saree in a tight wad into her mouth to try to silence the sobs.

'I've not yet been able to buy a good *thaavani* cloth for Sivakami to drape across her upper body. Everyone's been asking for a month now why Sivakami isn't yet wearing a *thaavani.* In fact, Chinna Kanakkaan seems to have remarked that Sivakami looked like a Malayalee chick because she was not wearing a *thaavani.* Then everyone laughed at his remark, and Sivakami was weeping when she told me about it that day at home. Wait, let the Company reopen….I won't rest in peace till I confront that fellow and throw some questions in his face. I will make him want to die of shame for the way he behaved. Any fellow with sisters would have better sense than to talk like that. Going around with their tongues hanging out, these fellows… looking to see which girl is showing what….'

The nagging rain appeared to have died away at last. Even though it was still only evening, the overcast sky made it look as if night was already approaching. Thangammal picked up a sack, folded it into a triangle and draped it on her head, and set off towards the Company. She passed the main gate of the match factory, turned into the ginning factory road, and approached the company office. She heard the sounds of movement from inside. She took the sack off her head, threw it under the sirissa tree that stood nearby, and peeped into the room. The company foreman was alone inside, moving the racks around.

'What's the matter, Thangam *Akka*, why are you here in this rain?'

'Isn't the boss here, *thambi*?'

'He was here a moment ago. He said he was going to the

small company....he has just left.'

'There's no money for food today, *thambi.* So I was hoping to ask the boss for twenty rupees as advance. If you have five rupees, please give it to me, *thambi.* I will give it back to you tomorrow when I get the advance.'

'I swear I don't have any money, *Akka.* If I did would I ever say no to you?'

'We starved in the afternoon also. Sivakami went and lay down feeling weak and exhausted. I don't know what to do about the night. Wherever I turn it is like hitting my head against a stone wall. The rain on top of everything else....'

'If you have any kind of tin, bring it, *Akka*. I will give you some flour. There isn't anyone else here right now. Go and make *dosais* or at least cook some *upma.*'

'But won't the flour have zinc mixed in it?'

'No, there is flour without zinc also.'

The foreman went inside and came out with a tin full of flour. He looked around furtively and then handed the tin to Thangammal.

'*Ey akka*, please don't tell anyone about this. If anyone comes to know....that will be the end of us. Even if someone asks, tell them you did not pick up the flour for the paste the other day so you are bringing it today. Don't forget to bring back the tin.'

Thangammal grabbed the tin, tucked it into the curve of her hip and pulled her saree folds over it. She picked up the sack from where she had left it under the sirissa tree, and came out into the street. The street lights were already on.

By the time Thangammal reached home, it was totally

dark. There was no light inside the house. She groped for the matchbox near the fireplace, and lit the lamp. Sivakami was still fast asleep.

'*Thaayi…emma*…Sivakami, get up. Come on, get up and wash your face. See, your Amma has bought some flour. Get up, my little princess.'

Sivakami awoke and sat up. Thangammal smoothed back her daughter's tangled hair and wiped her face vigorously with the edge of her saree. She ran the fingers of both hands through the girl's hair. Sivakami, now wide awake, looked up at her mother.

'The boss has gone to the small company. Before he leaves I will hurry over there and ask him for twenty rupees as advance. I will be back soon. I have brought some flour in the tin. Make some *upma* with it. If it gets too late it may start raining again and then it will be impossible for me to go. Come on, shake out the sack and throw it over the door. Put water on to boil. I will be back in no time.'

Thangammal picked up the head-cover sack again in case she needed it.

'How did you get the flour?'

'I had gone to the Company. The foreman *thambi* gave it to me.'

'If someone had seen you both, the foreman would be in trouble.'

'Nobody saw us, you fool. Don't talk so loudly. If some busybody hears you and spreads the news around, it will be goodbye to even this. Then you and I will be left with nothing…sitting around staring and picking our teeth.'

Thangammal hurried away without waiting for Sivakami's response. When Sivakami went to inspect the oil bottle, she found a glint of oil right at the bottom. The bottle was hanging by a wire from a nail in the wall, and the mouth of the bottle was stoppered with a small ball of tamarind. The sight of that gleam of oil in the bottle brought an answering gleam of joy to Sivakami's face. She opened the spice box. There lay four or five onions and some pieces of pale dry chillies. Sivakami was as elated as if her stomach was already half-full. She ran to the fireplace and reached for the matchbox to light the fire....

Thangammal stooped to enter the house so as to avoid hitting her head. She took the sack from under her arm where she had tucked it, and threw it into a corner. She looked around, and reeled back in shock. Her daughter Sivakami lay sprawled on the floor in a faint. She seemed to be murmuring inaudibly. Around her were puddles of vomit.

'*Adiye*! You accursed girl! What have you done! What did you eat, you wretch, tell me, what did you eat...?'

Sivakami's eyes were rolling wildy. She was muttering something, but the words were not clear. Thangammal lowered her daughter's head from her lap to the floor. She picked up the chimney-lamp and ran up the steps. The tin that she had brought home that evening from the foreman at the company, the tin that had the good flour without any zinc in it, lay untouched. She ran towards the fireplace. There lay the old tin that had held the zinc-mixed flour. Thangammal's head reeled.

'O you wretched, cursed witch, you devil, you have

turned my life to ashes. *Enthaayi…*'

The chimney-lamp slipped out of her hands. Slamming both hands repeatedly against her head, she ran out with her hair streaming wildly. There was a single pillar standing between floor and roof to prevent the sloping roof from sliding and falling. She collided hard against the pillar and fell to the floor. A loud lamentation and a heart-rending cry broke the stillness of the pitch-dark night. And a small moan. Apart from that, nothing.

Glossary

Thaayili!: exclamation expressing astonishment

josyam: fortune-telling.

josyakaarar: fortune-teller.

paavaadai: traditional waist-to-floor skirt worn by young girls.

thinnai: masonry platform in traditional houses, usually used for sitting or lying on, but occasionally as a work surface.

Aipasi, Karthigai: two months of the Tamil calendar year.

thaavani: a 'half-saree'; cloth half the length of a saree, tucked at the waist and worn draped across the bosom, traditionally worn by nubile, teenage girls in many parts of South India.

akka, thambi: literally, elder sister and younger brother, respectively; here used as familiar forms of address

dosai, upma: snack or 'tiffin' dishes in South India.

PONNAMMAI

KOVEDHA SWAMINATHAN

"Ey, Kannuppoochi… I've brought food, come and eat, all of you." Placing the food basket under the portia tree on the embankment of the well, Ponnammai called out to them. Her husband Karnan and her brothers-in-law, Vellaiyan, Poolan, Kuppaiyandi and Kannuppoochi were busy tilling the brinjal field. Millet seedlings were ready for cultivation. Vellaiyan was at the front with his plough. He was the burliest of the brothers. Vellaiyan was one to readily take responsibility for any task that came his way. Generally involved in all scuffles and arguments in the village, he was short tempered and belligerent. Karnan, the eldest brother, and the other three were quiet types, minding their own business. Only Karnan and Vellaiyan were married. Vellaiyan was planning to arrange the weddings of his three brothers in one go under the same roof. There was no arguing with him. The villagers called them the five *Pandavas*. However, the family's ways were such that Karnan

---

Translated by V Ramakrishnan

Original Source: 'Ponnammai': From *Dalit Sirukathai Thoguppu:* An Anthology of Dalit Short Stories compiled by P Sivakami (Sahitya Akademi, 2014)

was not analogous to *Dharman*.

"*Ey*, Kannuppoochi, come and have food," Ponnammai called out again.

"*Ey*, wait a while, *aatha*! We'll finish up this ploughing," Karnan yelled back.

The freshly-tilled soil was loose and wet. Brinjal roots and scutch grass lay uprooted. Earthworms shining like steel wires and little-finger-sized grubs floated around here and there. The scent of the tilled soil was comforting. Poking his bull in the back with a cane and holding the plough in position, Vellaiyan said:

"Look when she brings food! Is it breakfast or lunch? These women have no fear in them."

Karnan, who was ploughing behind Vellaiyan, said, "What's the fuss now? They have to clean up the house, heat up water and then cook, right?"

Poolan, who was coming behind Karnan, said, "*Anna*, what's the rush? If you're so hungry, why don't you rest the plough and go?"

"*Ey*, did I say I was hungry? If these women take so long to bring food to the fields, how long would they take if we worked in the foothill forest!" Vellaiyan replied.

"They'll come when they come. Both *madhinis* work all day long from dawn until nightfall without rest. Stop complaining and keep your bull moving, *na*," responded Kuppaiyandi.

Ponnammai came to the field through the canal.

"*Ey*, why don't you come soon? Finish your meal and come back to work. *Akka* has prepared a delicious meat stew. Also, *kali* is good when consumed hot," she reminded them.

"Wait just a few minutes, *madhini*... We'll plough just this line and come. You go, the crows might come for the food basket," Kannuppoochi said.

Over a dozen crows were perched on the portia tree's branch. Ponnammai hurried back to the embankment. Vellaiyan did not utter a word. Holding down the plough, he hit the bull hard and drove it forward.

"*Ey*, what's wrong with you? You're the first in the line of ploughs, and you're hitting the bull too hard. Won't it get agitated?" Karnan admonished him.

Just as he said, the red bull on the right lurched, terrified. The beam had slipped from over its neck. Vellaiyan slackened the plough and set the beam back up on its neck.

The crows on the portia tree apprehensively watched Ponnammai running towards them. It didn't look like Vellaiyan was going to stop ploughing anytime soon. Realizing that her husband and her brothers-in-law were too engrossed in their work to think about food, Ponnammai hesitated to call out to them again. She went down the well to wash herself up. She jumped into the water, swam gaily for a while, and with her saree dripping wet, came back up to the embankment. She wrung out the end of her saree, tied it to one of the lower branches of the tree and stood there, letting it dry in the air. This only infuriated Vellaiyan a little more.

"*Ey*, how you make a living with this lady! We men are working here, and look at her standing there shamelessly after a dunk in the well! How is she going to serve us food if we go there now?" Vellaiyan asked Karnan irritably.

"What's wrong with that now? Let's help ourselves to the food. It is common for women in her village to take a dip and swim in ponds and wells. It's just that habit," Karnan defended his wife.

"Let her keep those habits to her village. When she's here, she has to shower only where women are supposed to. She must not stand there shamelessly like that, baring everything to anyone who passes by. What would people think of us!"

Karnan did not respond. He was afraid that another word in support of his wife would earn a sound beating from Vellaiyan for himself and for his brothers who would invariably try to protect him. Vellaiyan stopped ploughing and looked back at his brothers.

"Go, all of you! The lady from the foreign land has passed water in the well. You men go and drink it," he said hotly.

"*Dei*, listen! A shameless being like her must not be part of our household. You are going to take her to her parents' place tomorrow and leave her there. Or, if she's the most important thing to you, you too stay there. Keep your business there. I must not see her at home tomorrow," he spoke severely to Karnan.

No one had the courage to speak against their angry brother. Vellaiyan, meanwhile, released the harness, took the bulls to their shed, tied them there, and headed home.

When the brothers went to the embankment to have

their meal, Ponnammai asked them, "Why did your brother walk away angrily without eating?"

"He's gone mad all of a sudden," Kannuppoochi replied.

When she looked at her husband, he said, "It's my fate!"

"Whatever you mean by fate! Anyway, you all have your meal," she said, serving *ragi kali* with meat stew. The crows shifted restlessly on the portia tree's branch and cawed.

* * *

That night, before going to bed, Ponnammai said, "Why did your brother walk away so angrily today? *Akka* prepared steaming *kali* for him knowing he loves it. I brought it to the field in a hurry, you know. I feel bad that he went without eating it."

"Forget that. We have not seen your parents in a long time. It's been about six months, right? The last time we visited them was when Veluthayi came of age. Shall we go to Paalur tomorrow and stay there for a week?" he asked as if he had not heard her.

"I would love that. The image of Veluthayi is still in my eyes. I keep thinking of her. Let's go. But wouldn't the work here come to a stop if we leave? Your brother said you're cultivating next week... Why don't we go after the cultivation?" she asked.

"It'll take time. The seedlings will have to grow a few more inches. We will be back before then. You better pack your clothes and be ready. Let's start early before dawn" he replied.

"I don't think I'll get a wink of sleep tonight," she said, and went to Vellaiyan's wife, Rasathi, and the rest of the family members to inform them that she would be leaving for her village the next day.

"*Ey*, why the sudden plan? There is work piled up in the field, and you're telling me you're leaving tomorrow," Rasathi enquired.

"I told him that, *akka*. But he says we have to leave right away," she said.

Rasathi did not ask Karnan about the sudden plan. She just stayed quiet. Thrilled by the prospect of seeing her village, the familiar streets where she had played as a child, the fields where she had worked, the ponds and wells in which she had spent several playful hours, and thinking about meeting her friends again, Ponnammai could not catch a wink that night. She lay with her arm on her husband's chest, eyes closed, nowhere near falling asleep.

* * *

They got off at Paalur the next morning at around 11. Even as they got off the bus, Ponnammai's eyes bored through the tamarind trees in the distance, eager to sight her village and her house. She was looking for a familiar face on the way from the bus stop to her village. There was none. Her house was not far from the bus stop. Karnan and Ponnammai took the channel that led to the village. Veluthayi, who had been outside the house, had spotted them the moment they got off the bus.

"*Ey*, *akka* and *mama* are coming," she shouted out to her mother and ran to meet them. Seeing her younger sister come towards her, Ponnammai left her husband behind and rushed forward. She clutched Veluthayi's hands and asked after her health, and caressed her shoulders and head affectionately. Veluthayi took the bag from her sister's hands and held it to her waist. Her body reflected the sheen of her youth. There was excitement and innocence bubbling on her face.

"Velu, *athai* and *mama* are fine, right?" Karnan inquired.

"Yes, *macchaan*."

Veluthayi walked towards the house like a frolicking lamb, chatting with her sister and brother-in-law. Alamelu had come to the mouth of the channel to receive her daughter and son-in-law. Neighbours who had heard of the couple's arrival were also gathered by this time. After all, wasn't Ponnammai the girl who was married into a well off family in the west? No one had expected her to be transformed, in just eight months since her wedding, into such a pretty, mature and bright lady, like a gleaming banana plant growing on fertile soil. Other girls in Ponnammai's family, who also longed to be married off to the west, entered into conversation with Karnan.

"*Ey*, *macchaan*. It's been eight months, and we see no sign of anything. We were thinking you had brought her here for her third trimester!"

Karnan smiled without uttering a word. Since his parents-in-law were also in the foyer, he felt quite shy. He stood washing his face outside the entrance.

"*Ey*, shut it, girls! Let them eat something. Trying to pull words out of their mouths already..." Alamelu chided them.

***

Karnan stayed at Paalur for two days. Then, saying that he would come and take Ponnammai back after a month, he left for his village.

Ponnammai did not even attempt to ask her husband, "What is this? You told me we were staying for a week, but you're leaving me here now!" The naive girl had such faith in her husband's words. Karnan did not listen to the entreaties of Alamelu, Periya Naachan and Veluthaayi. All of them went to the bus stop to send him off. Ponnammai walked all the way, holding Karnan's hands lovingly.

"Please come soon and take me with you, *macchaan*. I can't sleep properly without you. Food won't stay in my body either," cried Ponnammai when he boarded the bus. She waited there until the smoke-billowing bus disappeared from her sight, and only then turned to walk towards her home. That was the last they saw of him. Days, weeks, months and years rolled by. Neither Karnan nor his brothers nor Rasathi came to take her back. It had all ended like a dream. Periya Naachan took considerable efforts to reunite the couple.

"I can't live with that traitor again after he betrayed me so inhumanly. If you try bringing us together again, you won't see me alive," Ponnammai declared resolutely.

Periya Naachan gave up after this. Time, on the other hand, gave in to no one's pleas, and kept flying at the pace of a whirlwind.

* * *

Periya Naachan died when Ponnammai was twenty-five. He was bitten by a viper when he had gone to Vaalikkaradu to collect prickly pears—he fainted and died on the way home. Alamelu joined him soon after that. She had gone to work in the fields despite the heavy rains; and come down with a fever. She died in her bed after suffering a violent bout of fits. In death, she looked like a cow lying in its shed with stiffened legs. Ponnammai's elder brother, Anaikkaraiyan, who had gone to procure fertilizers, died like a felled coconut tree when a wooden shed collapsed on his neck. His four daughters held Ponnammai's legs and wept bitterly. Veluthayi was the only remaining solace for Ponnammai. But on one occasion when they had a fight, Veluthayi's husband, Mayilan, kicked her in the stomach. She became bedridden after that and suffered inexpressible pain for the next six months. Without any money to consult a doctor, she resorted to consuming herbs from near streams and ponds, and died, her body bloated. Her husband and three children were left shell shocked by the sudden blow.

Ponnammai started toiling for the sake of both her brother's and her sister's children. The children grew up and left the household after they found their respective spouses in different directions. She no longer had anyone whom she could call family in the village. She lived like an orphan in the house left to her by her dead parents—in the village where she had grown up nurturing many dreams. She bought a few goats and reared them. But since she could not cope with the efforts involved in goat-rearing, she sold them. She then bought a dozen sheep. But it was difficult to find fodder for them in the rainy season. A few of them died due to some kind of fever.

Knowing well that no one would come to the aid of the lonely woman, thieves, both from within the village and other villages, took away some sheep when they were grazing near the stream. Ponnammai grew tired of expecting any sign of humanity in the people around her. She sold the rest of her sheep and resigned to a quiet life.

She lost her strength as she aged. The grit in her heart was drying up. However, she did not wish to be a burden to anyone. With a basket tucked under her arm, she would follow the grazing cows, collect their dung, make dried dung-cakes for fuel, and sell them. She would also strip the barks of the roadside tamarind trees and supply them to Ramu Devan's tea shop. He gave her a cup of tea in return. He also gave her some unsold *vadais*, and occasionally, five or ten rupees. She would make porridge three times a week and have it over a week. Thus went her days.

* * *

Ponnammai is about seventy-five years old now. She has wrinkled skin, veins standing out on her emaciated arms, and cotton-white hair. Looking past her rheumy eyes one can see how her brows droop. She has started using a cane for support. Her life runs on a bowl of porridge or a gulp of liquid food. She doesn't recall many things that happened in the past, both good and bad. Occasionally, a memory would descend like a bolt of lightning. Once in a while, she would go to the bus stop. Children playing in the shade of the tamarind tree there would mock her.

"*Ey*, old lady! Look, the bus that goes to your husband's

village is here. Are you going?"

"Hit you with my slippers! How dare you ask me if I'm going to that traitor's place! I have dignity, you know... I'm dignified..." She would chase away the children with the cane in her hand.

"*Ey*, crazy lady *da*..." the children would run away shouting.

Ponnammai *is* crazy, isn't she?

Glossary

madhini - sister-in-law

ragi kali - a pasty pudding made from finger millet

vadai – fritter

STREET THEATRE

V VENKATACHALAM

There was a time when dust swirled through the street under the feet of cattle and sheep returning after grazing their fill. Long after the kerosene lamps had been lit, the sounds of hoof beats would linger on. Marking the passage of the animals, the street was liberally stained with cow urine, dung and sheep droppings. In those days, when the yield from the fields had ushered in a measure of prosperity, Ponnu Vadhiyaar's *koothu* performances were very popular in and around the village.

Ponnu, who had studied up to class eight, knew the Mahabharatam, together with all the supplementary stories, at his fingertips. With the advent of the month of *Panguni* every year, organisers from the Draupadi temples around the area would seek him out to perform an eighteen-day Mahabharatham session. Hair liberally oiled and cascading in curly waves onto his shoulders, neat stripes of *vibhuti* across his forehead, and lips moist with fresh betel juice, he cut a fine figure as an artiste.

Translated by Malini Seshadri

Original Source: 'Koothu', *Dalit Sirukathai Thoguppu:* An Anthology of Dalit Short Stories compiled by P Sivakami (Sahitya Akademi, 2014)

He was the owner of some dry farm land and half a dozen sheep. In his opinion, working on the land, watering, tilling, sowing—all these were tasks for lesser mortals. Once the *koothu* season was over, he would take his sheep into a grassy area in the woods and leave them to graze while he perched atop a mound of boulders. In that felicitous setting, he would launch into song at a high pitch, practising different kinds of compositions and ironing out imperfections. Even in the midst of everyday activities, he could be seen muttering *koothu*-related dialogues under his breath.

With stiff boards tied onto his shoulders to broaden them and a crown placed majestically on his head, he became the very embodiment of Duryodhanan, descendant of the Kaurava lineage that ruled Hastinapura, right down to the regal gait and the distinctive voice. Appearing quite shy and timid at normal times, Ponnu's voice would acquire a deep timbre whenever he took on the persona of a hero for his performances. And when he took on a female role, that same voice would transform magically into softness, like the shimmer of gold coins. Whenever he launched into a leisurely raga essay as a prelude to a song, even those rushing by in a hurry to get somewhere would pause to take in the melody. During tragic scenes, he would pull the end of his sari costume over his face and sob aloud; and the women in the audience would weep and sniffle with him. The grief he portrayed could sway even the men. The words of his songs emerged clear as crystal from his lips. As an example, this song from 'Karnan Moksham' in the scene depicting Karnan's wife Ponnuruvi in the royal court:

Thagitthom thagitthom thai... naagarathinam minnuthe...barithi vadivaiotha...ponnurivi maadhu vandhen. Thagitthom thagitthom thai... (Oh how the snake-gems gleam and shine... Like the blazing sun itself... Here I come... I, woman, I, Ponnurivi.)

The man who had once moved around briskly befitting the outstanding artiste he was had now turned into an anaemic, pale shadow of his former self. For the past twenty years or so, whenever anyone asked, 'What's happening, Vadhyar? Not performing in any dramas these days?', Ponnu would respond with a wry smile, as though to say, 'Which fellow is willing nowadays to stay awake at night to watch a *koothu*? It's been a world of video cassettes and cable TV for a long time now.' The real reason stayed hidden. Occasionally, under the influence of liquor, he would open up if someone were to probe; then he would reveal his artiste's soul and the true meaning behind the wry smile.

Ponnu Vadhyar was busy mixing oilcake in cool water, preparing feed for the sheep he had bought on loan. He spotted Thimman approaching, and a smile broke out on his face, which had not felt the touch of theatre make-up for many years. He gestured to Thimman to go and sit on the rock adjoining his house. Ponnu's wife, who had been squatting on the floor and grinding masala on the grinding stone in the verandah, paused in her work. Getting up as though to clear away some dead leaves that had fallen off the roof tiles, she cast an oblique glance at Thimman. She seemed to have worked out the reason for his visit, because she was very annoyed.

'Well, machaan...what brings you all this way?' asked Ponnu.

'Oh, just dropping in, that's all, Vadhyar,' said Thimman. 'Finished plucking all the beans?'

'What's the use? A couple of beans on each plant....No rain. If this happens again next year, well...it would be utter ruin....'

As he was talking Thimman extracted the liquor bottle he had hidden under his shirt, and placed it carefully on the rock. He had also brought along a snack of salted beef, lightly fried with spices and roughly pounded on a grinding stone. The country liquor went down very comfortably.

'Vadhyar, we must put up a *koothu* performance in our village. I will get a 'set' ready, and you do the koothu.

'No, no, Thimma, let us not do that. You know what they say, seeds sown for mere pride will only turn into grass for the buffaloes.'

'Don't think this is just some drunken talk, Vadhyar. Once evening set in, our streets used to be so full of happy bustle.... singing, dancing....remember? Now everyone is huddled indoors in front of their TVs. Ever since the day that Murugesan fellow connected up the cable lines for TV, even the children do nothing but sit and stare at the screen. School children don't seem to be opening their books any more. Where are the sounds of the ABCs, the recitations...? Bad enough that our generation had no education and so we have made nothing of our lives. When we were hoping that our children at least would study and get ahead in life, this accursed cable TV has come and is killing those dreams. If we are to lure them away from TV, the only way is through organising *koothus*. Will you agree to teach us? What do you say?'

'Teaching...is there a koothu dance I haven't taught? A role I haven't played? When I played Veeman, I would roll my eyes, leap around, jiggle my body and roar "Through all the eons of time, I come *gidir gidir*.....through all the worlds I shine *gubir gubir*...". Even the little children who did not understand would be so excited they would wet their pants.' By now Ponnu's enthusiasm had climbed high. He proceeded to confide in Theeman a secret from his days as a *koothu* artiste.

Just next to Ponnu's village runs the Krishnagiri Bangalore national highway. If one were to walk along this highway, the village of Ottaiyanur lies just beyond the second kilometre marker stone. Back in the day when he was still young and full of vigour, Ponnu had agreed to teach *koothu* to the young boys of that village. After working in the fields, tending to his sheep and preparing something to eat, he would set off walking to Ottaiyanur at about seven in the evening, and get back around midnight. In those days when forest folk with wild, matted hair moved around at night, earthen oil pots on their heads and dirty cloth bundles at their waists, it was no simple matter for a lone man to venture on to that road at that hour. On the onward journey to Ottaiyanur it was still early enough in the evening and so there were some people still around. But on his way back home, he would have his heart in his mouth till he reached old Madarasu's shop, just a shouting distance from his village. It was rumoured that a pale ghost would stand there and scream 'Ayyo! Amma!' It was said that it had recognized a man by his footfall, and had crushed and snapped his neck so that he vomited blood and fell dead. Stories like these swirled in his mind and filled him with dread.

Somehow he managed to finish teaching them the play 'Thapasu' (Penance). In order to ensure there were no blunders, he himself took on the main role of Arjunan. A huge crowd turned up to watch. Ponnu, with a mat made of split bamboo and peacock feathers strapped to his back, launched into a kavadi*-like dance en route to his penance in his persona as Arjuna. As he swayed and danced, he sang:

Thapasukku naaanum poga-----naanum poga

Linga poojai naanum seidhen----linga poojai---naanum seidhen

Om Arakara Mahadeva

I go to offer penance... To do penance I go..

I offered prayers to the linga...the linga...the linga I did worship

Om Arakara Mahadeva

As Ponnu swirled and danced, appreciative roars of 'Sivo Jayam' (All hail to Siva) broke out in the audience, and coins rained down all around him. Later, when he had moved behind the stage to smoke a *beedi*, a woman who had been watching him came running forward. She embraced and kissed him, and then vanished as rapidly as she had come before he could even think of asking who she was.

Next Ponnu agreed to teach the youth the tragic play about Keechakan from the Virata Parvam (Fourth part of the Mahabharata). The very first day, as he crossed Madarasu's shop, he saw the tall figure of a woman dressed all in white. She started following him. At a point just after where the tar road sloped downwards, she started walking faster and caught up to him. She continued to walk at his side. Ponnu thought to himself, 'A woman all alone at this late hour. We can be company for each other on the way'. As they walked along, neither of them turned to glance at the other.

'Where are you going, ma?' asked Ponnu.

'Where are you headed to?' she responded, speaking in Kannada.

Ponnu replied in Kannada. 'I'm going to Ottaiyanur.'

'I too am going there,' declared the woman.

Then, 'Please give me a bit of tobacco to chew,' she asked.

'Sorry, I don't have any.'

She speaks Kannada, thought Ponnu to himself. She must be a Kurumba tribal woman from Ottaiyanur.

Many doubts and suspicions about her started sprouting in his mind. Could she be a mad woman? Just then a lorry approached, and in its headlights Ponnu could see an elderly man approaching, leaning on a cane as he walked along. At the same time, the woman darted behind a roadside banyan tree as though to relieve herself. She didn't emerge for quite some time. Only then was Ponnu struck by the chilling revelation that she was no flesh-and-blood woman. The pit of his stomach turned to ice, and he broke into a violent sweat. That night he did not take the trip back home, but decided to stay the night at the village he was visiting.

For several days afterwards he would not even sleep with his head facing in the direction of his encounter with the mysterious woman. But the youth of the neighbouring village were persistent. They came repeatedly and nagged him to finish what he had agreed to do. He was forced to restart the interrupted lessons. Sure enough, as he crossed the Madarasu's shop the woman appeared and started walking with him. He talked himself into an attitude of bravado. 'She wants to walk, so let her walk,' he told himself. And so the pattern was set. Every day she would walk with him from the shop to the banyan tree, at which point she would disappear behind the tree and not emerge again.

Old Madarasu's shop was a little bit away from the side of the tar road. The talk in the village was that he used to live in Chennai, and had moved with his family to Mysore to try to earn a living. There he caught his wife having an affair with another man. He finished her off and moved to the outskirts of Ottaiyanur where he set up a small shop at the side of the highway. A grown daughter was also said to live with him. A few yards away stood a banyan tree, and it was from there that the woman would emerge when Ponnu passed by and fall into step with him. On the way back, there would be absolutely no hint of her presence around the tree.

As the days passed, Ponnu and she grew close. He was careful not to upset her in any way. She sometimes brought buns and biscuits to eat along the way. When he asked her where she had got them, she would say she stole them from Madarasu's shop. In fact, whatever Ponnu requested her to bring, she somehow managed to do, even when it entailed difficulties. She even helped out with money now and then in emergencies. After a while, Ponnu got into the habit of setting out for the day's *koothu* lesson only to indulge in a leisurely chat with the woman along the way and return home directly after she disappeared behind the tree. Their interactions grew from mere minutes to several hours. He mesmerised her with his *koothu* songs, stories and *keerthanams*. Their intimacy grew deep. One day, she asked him to fulfil a perverse desire of hers. Her suggestion that they should enter into a sexual relationship did not shock Ponnu as may have been expected. He indicated that he was of the same mind, and he left the planning of the where and when to her. Later, brimming with excitement, she announced that she had selected a new moon day; Ponnu agreed it was a perfect choice. Both awaited the arrival of the appointed day, dreaming their special dreams.

The selected day arrived. There was a disused threshing shed behind the bushes that bordered the road, and that was where they met. She had brought plenty of eats tied up as a bundle in her sari. In the deepening darkness he laid his head on her lap. As they talked Ponnu's hands moved over her body, arousing secret desires. As passions flamed, shirt buttons were ripped off and strewn. They were about to consummate their union when a gleam of light appeared. Old Madarasu stood there, lantern in hand.

The old man's body was trembling like a plucked *tanpura* string. His breath grew ragged as his fury rose. His face took on a frightening expression, and even the hairs on his head seemed to stand on end. He screamed like a tortured spirit.

'You have descended to consorting with a low-caste *koothu* fellow. You deserve to be killed.' As he shouted he wielded the bamboo cane he had brought with him, swinging it and striking her repeatedly and mercilessly. A heartbroken Ponnu crept away. When he turned to look, he could see dimly through the murky light that the old man was dragging her away.

For the next one week, Ponnu did not venture in that direction. It was only when he went there later that he heard what had happened. She was supposed to have died after being hit by a lorry on the road. The old man had quietly and discreetly taken care of everything without even the neighbouring village hearing anything of it. Ponnu ran back to his village in great agitation and blurted out this news. Everyone pretended no such thing had ever happened.

Having come to the end of his story, Ponnu's eyes were brimming with unshed tears. Thimman had fallen asleep halfway through. A stray dog was licking the paper wrapping that had held Thimman's snack.

'It's very late. Enough of all the story-telling. You start drinking and you forget you have a wife and family,' scolded Ponnu's wife as she walked towards him.

Glossary

Koothu: Traditional street theatre with drama, song and dance
Panguni: Last month of the Tamil calendar
Draupadi: An important female character in the Mahabharatha
Mahabharatham: Ancient Indian epic
Vibhuti: Sacred ash, often smeared on the forehead
Karnan moksham: A scene from the Mahabharatham in which the Character Karnan from the Mahabharatham dies
Arjunan: One of the most important characters in the Mahabharatham
Kavadi: Ceremonial dance as part of penance offering to the God, Murugan
Linga/Lingam: Stone representation of Lord Shiva, worshipped in temples
Beedi: Cheap hand-rolled cheroot
Keechakan: A character in the Mahabharatham
Kurumba: The name of a tribe inhabiting that area
Keerthanam: A classical music composition
Tanpura: A stringed musical instrument to set the pitch+

BHOGI HAS COME AND GONE

GOWTHAMA SANNAH

"Aarogyam, stand up. Mm, tell me, which festival comes the day before Pongal?"

"Bhoyi, teacher."

"Not 'bhoyi', da. Say 'bhogi'. Right, now recite the homework I gave you all yesterday."

"Bhogi festival is the day before Pongal. As the village song goes, it is for getting rid of the old and bringing in the new. So we burn all the old clothes, mats and other such things in the house and prepare ourselves to start anew. Also,...."

"Enough...stop. Were you boys listening? What is Bhogi?"

The boys echoed Aarogyam's words in a loud chorus.

"That's right. Now today is Friday. Saturday and Sunday are school holidays. Bhogi is on Monday. The next school day after today will be only next Thursday. Now all of you start reading the lesson 'Pongal O Pongal'. *De*, Kumar...

Translated by Malini Seshadri

Original Source: Bhogiyum Pochi, *Dalit Sirukathai Thoguppu*: An Anthology of Dalit Short Stories compiled by P Sivakami (Sahitya Akademi, 2014) stand up. Write down the names of anyone who talks."

The teacher left the room. The boys could not keep silent as they had been ordered to do. They were eager to share their dreams of the approaching Pongal day and the prospect of new clothes. Kumar too was tempted to join in, but the monitoring assignment the teacher had given him held him back.

"*De*, Aarogyam, what are you going to do on Bhogi?" whispered Saravanan who was sharing the bench.

"Oh, that...well I've already collected waste shrubs and weeds and scattered them on the roof of my house to dry. Today I will have to go and find some old tyres and rubber chappals. That's important for keeping the Bhogi fire going for a long time. Okay, quiet now...Kumar is looking our way..."

Kumar warned, "*De*, Saravana, keep quiet. Otherwise I will write your name. Got it?"

The teacher returned. "Did anyone talk?"

"No, teacher. No one."

The teacher picked up her handbag and left for the day.

***

Aarogyam went home. He hung up his school bag on the stand and set off to find tyres and rubber chappals. After dark, he returned with four bicycle tyres and ten to fifteen chappals, all of them threaded through with a rope for easier transport.

Amma was angry. "You donkey!" she shouted. "There's already such a pile of shrubs and weeds. Wasn't that enough for Bhogi? Now you've gone and collected all these tyres and chappals as well..."

Aarogyam tossed the tyres and chappals onto the roof. Then he washed his hands and feet and settled down to his lessons.

"*De.* You good-for-nothing...why did you throw the tyres onto the roof? Already the house is tilting to one side...I'm so worried that it's going to fall over completely one of these days. Take them off the roof, *da.*"

"No, Amma, let them be there. If they are left on the ground somebody may steal them."

"Oh, why does this wretched Bhogi come at all! This fellow causes me such a bother....brings all the wild plants from all over town and throws them on the roof to dry. Okay, your father has bought a drum for you. Go and play it...not right here, go somewhere else...."

At the corner of the cooking platform lay a small drum of the kind traditionally made for children.

Aarogyam was reminded of what his teacher had taught them at school. 'On Bhogi day children beat their drums as they dance around the bonfire.' He picked up the drum and hurried away in search of his friends.

The coming dawn would bring Bhogi day. Against a clear sky, a cloud of mist swirled around. It did not spare the hutments. Through the cracks it entered Aarogyam's hut too and ran as droplets of water down the walls. As the boy lay dreaming of Bhogi, wrapped in an old gunny sack for warmth with his leg sticking out through a hole in the sack, the cold mist settled wetly on his exposed leg.

At about four in the morning, Amma woke Aarogyam. '*De*, get up...go and look outside..everyone is already starting the Bhogi fires.'

Aarogyam's dream dissolved abruptly; he jumped up and ran outside. The 'Dum..Dum' of the boys' drums banished any lingering drowsiness.

He quickly pulled down all the old things that had been lying on the roof. He took some of them aside and fetched a kerosene lamp. He poured out some kerosene on the pile and set it alight. Aarogyam's Bhogi bonfire flared and flamed.

He picked up the drum. Dum...dum..dum he banged on it as he circled the bonfire. His friends in the neighbouring huts woke at the sound of the drums and ran to join him.

As they pranced around the fire, the boys sang the very same song that their forefathers had sung on Bhogi day.

Bhogi is gone
And Pongal too
Give me your girl
Machaan...

They all sang in chorus. Then Aarogyam sang solo:

Turmeric plant...Flowering plant...

The chorus joined in. Then:

"*Any ghost that comes here*
will get thrashed with slippers"

In the space of just an hour, all the dried shrubs and rubber chappals that Aarogyam had collected over a whole month were consumed by the flames. Only half a dozen old bicycle tyres were left. The boys lit up one of the tires and started out with it on their Bhogi procession.

Aarogyam led the way. The rest followed, singing

snatches of folk songs in a gaggle of voices. They sang them multiple times. And then they moved on to film songs.

By the time they had circled the *cheri* ten to fifteen times, many more boys had joined and the procession had grown very long. By the time all the tires were burnt to ashes one by one, the dawn was breaking.

In the early morning light, the world appeared steeped in thick smoke. Any stranger coming by would have thought the *cheri* folk were prosperous. After all, a whole lot of old clothes, pillows, mats and other household things must have been burnt to produce this much smoke!

Aarogyam went home half-asleep. But the hot black tea laced with jaggery that his mother had bought for him drove away all vestiges of sleep.

He recalled his school lesson about Pongal. On the day before Pongal, that is, Bhogi, all the old things in the house must be burnt. Right, that part of it was done. But then one had to clean the house, whitewash the walls and make pretty *kolam* patterns on the floor.

"Mma, when are you planning to clean the house and whitewash the walls?"

"De, it's clean enough as it is. Any more cleaning will disturb the dried palm leaves on the roof and the holes will get larger. Instead, look....I'm cleaning some of the things..."

"Oh, all right. But at least let us do the whitewashing."

"Whitewash..nightwash..all that is only for houses with proper walls, da. It can't be done in our kind of house with thatch on all sides. Go...go and play."

Aarogyam's face fell. "Amma, our teacher said we should

burn all the old clothes and other old things in the house. Have you finished doing that?"

Amma did not reply.

Aarogyam was very sad as he went outside. The 'new' clothes he would get every Pongal day were the hand-me-downs of the children in the house where his mother worked. Or else, used clothes from a shop in Parrys Corner.

This Pongal, the clothes were from Parrys Corner. Since they were new to him, Aarogyam did not understand that they were actually old. The smell of camphor wafting from them was, to his mind, the smell of newness.

Amma made *dosais* and channa dal chutney for Pongal. This was the only special festival treat. Throughout the cheri, this was the festival fare for all three days of Pongal. A few who were slightly better off would also make *adirasam*. Some neighbours had sent *adirasam* to Aarogyam's home.

"Amma, why don't you also make *adirasam*?" pleaded Aarogyam, his voice filled with longing.

"Next time...just eat now."

The Pongal break of three days went by, bringing its quota of joys and sorrows. The children returned to school... those who had been able to wear new clothes, those who had worn second-hand Parrys Corner clothes, and some who had had to wear their own old clothes again.

The teacher was in a brand new silk sari, resplendent like Mahalakshmi.

"Now all of you must take turns to say what special food you ate for Pongal. You first, Kanaka..."

"*Dosai* and *curry sambar*, Teacher."

"Suresh...?"

"*Idli* and *curry sambar*, Teacher."

All the children mentioned either *idli* and *dosai* with *sambar*. A few added *adirasam* also.

The teacher was surprised. In her experience, *idlis* and *dosais* were everyday breakfast dishes, not festival fare.

"All right. What did you all burn on Bhogi day? Aarogyam, you start first."

"I had collected weeds and shrubs for fifteen days and spread them on our roof to dry. Then I went and found some old bicycle tyres and rubber *chappals*."

"Aiyaiyo! Rubber smoke can cause TB. Wasn't there any other old stuff in your house?"

"Teacher, I asked Amma. She said, if you are talking of old things, our house itself is old. Do you want to burn it also?"

The class burst into laughter. All this was new to the educated middle-class teacher who was alien to the reality of *cheri* life. Yet, with no realisation that her educated status had distanced her from society's realities, she felt no empathy for her wards. She plunged into the day's prescribed lesson.

"Right, last week I taught all of you the lesson on Bhogi. Aarogyam, can you remember it? Tell me...."

Aarogyam stood. "The Bhogi festival is on the day before Pongal. As the village song goes, it is for getting rid of the old and bringing in the new. So we burn all the old clothes, mats and other such things in the house and prepare ourselves to start anew. Also,...."

As he mouthed the words, his mind's eye saw a vivid picture of burning tires and chappals.

All the children in the class were bent over their books, following the lesson.

Glossary

Pongal: An important January festival in many parts of South India to celebrate the harvest
Bhogi: The day before Pongal day, involving customary cleansing Rituals
Machaan: A familiar form of mutual address between young men/boys
Kolam: An aesthetic pattern drawn on a floor or other surface, traditionally with rice floor. Associated with festivals.
Cheri: Slum settlement, particularly in an urban setting
Dosai: Traditional South Indian dish made of fermented batter of rice and lentils
Adirasam: A sweet snack for festivals, made with jaggery
Mahalakshmi: Hindu goddess
Sambar: Tamarind-based curry
Idli: Traditional steamed dish in South Indian cuisine, made from fermented rice and lentil batter

FOR A HANDFUL OF RICE

ABIMANI

"*Emmov*... Maasaanam here!" he would call in a sing-song voice from the front of the house. The women indoors would immediately bring two handfuls of cooked rice on a plate and put it in Maasaanam's bag or vessel. He would then move to the next house. His call would be heard: "*Emmov*... Maasaanam here!"

He was lean as a needle; more than half his hair had turned grey; he sported a beard, and his skin was wrinkled, showing his age. The four-yard dhoti he wore always looked shabby. He wore no shirt—the habit of wearing a shirt had gone with his youth. He always had a towel wound around his head. A little parcel of powdered tobacco would be wrapped in the dhoti around his waist. Whenever he felt a tingle in his mouth, he would unpack the parcel, take a couple of pinches of the powder, and apply it on his teeth for refreshment. That is what gave him the energy to go to

---

Translated by V Ramakrishnan
Original Source: Oorchoru, *Dalit Sirukathai Thoguppu*: An Anthology of Dalit Short Stories compiled by P Sivakami (Sahitya Akademi, 2014)

every house in the street to collect food. Not all houses may have food cooked and ready. In some homes, the rice pot would have just been placed on the stove. On such occasions, the voice from within the house would say, "Come after some time, *pa*. I've just set the pot for cooking." Annoyed, Maasaanam would move on to the next house, grumbling under his breath.

He would be exhausted by the time he had collected food from all the fifty-odd houses on that street—only a handful of those houses had tiled roofs; the rest had thatched roofs. He would not get rice from all the houses either. In some houses, he might get just corn or millet gruel. His conscience never let him reject any kind of food. He would find comfort in the thought that he got a small portion of what those householders themselves had. He wouldn't mind all kinds of food getting mixed up in his vessel. Once he reached home, he would ask his daughter-in-law to make a chutney, dilute the food he collected that day to the consistency of a porridge, and pour it into separate vessels for his son, daughter-in-law and grandson. If the chutney prepared that day was a little spicy, it would go perfectly with the porridge.

What else could they do? His family relied on that *oorchoru*. That street's laundry had been assigned to his family from his grandfather's days. He was responsible for collecting dirty laundry from all the houses once every week, steam bleach them, carry them to the Hanuman river shore in two to three bundles on his donkey, wash them on stones, dry them, bring them back home within a couple of days, and deliver them precisely to their respective houses. He was able to finish the laundry work only with the help of his son and his daughter-in-law. At his age, he found it difficult to manage all these tasks by himself. As long as his wife Baalamma, who died of a bloated stomach eleven years ago, had been with him, he had not needed anyone else's support in his work. Even if it were four huge bundles, the two used to wash them all quickly and get home in time. Today, however, he had to rely on his only son and his daughter-in-law—the couple had been married for three years now and had a two-year-old child. On days when there was no laundry to be done, the son and his wife would go to work in the field; the money they earned from such work was what helped them buy the necessary provisions for making gravy or chutney. When Maasaanam was late to return home after collecting *oorchoru* on some days, it was that money that helped the rest of the family alleviate their hunger.

His son has tried convincing his father several times: "Let's not be stuck with this job, *pa*. Why suffer with the donkeys, wash the filth of others, and live on the food they give? Why can't we work in the fields of the landlords like others do and earn from that?"

Maasaanam would reply, "Don't talk crazy *la*! We wash their clothes, and get food in return. How can we suddenly give up the occupation we've been doing for generations!"

Maasaanam knew it was not just every day's food that he got from the people of that street. He also earned six *padis* (approximately 8 kg) of paddy and fifty rupees every six months. With changing times, the compensation he got also went up, and yet it was not sufficient for him to raise his living standards. Theirs was still a hand-to-mouth existence. Unsurprisingly, he had nothing, apart from the house he had built and the two donkeys, to show as his accomplishments. Sometimes he would feel that the bleach stove that stood with its mouth wide open in front of his house in the east corner had gobbled up his life. If sparks exploding from the stove landed on them, the resulting irritation on the skin was unbearable—like centipedes crawling on the skin. The dirty laundry collected from the street houses on the previous day would be heaped in a mound in the thatched hut next to their house. Within the next couple of days, they would have to be bleached and taken to the river for washing.

His plight worsened when the river dried up. The wretched Hanuman river stood dry almost half the year. Flooding only during the rainy season, the river usually lay as a vast stretch of sand in summer. In such times, he went in search of a canal near a field along with the laden donkey. Even if he found a canal where he could wash the clothes, he would have to be wary of landlords who might yell, saying, "Ey Maasaanam, don't wash all kinds of dirt here and spoil the crops!" If the laundry was delayed because of such obstacles, the people in the street would row with him. He sometimes felt exasperated with his miserable lifestyle, but he consoled himself saying there was no other job he could do for his livelihood. On gloomy days like that, it was the tobacco powder that helped him regain composure: just two pinches applied behind his teeth would restore him to his lively self.

"*Emmov*... Maasaanam here!"

This was the last house. He called out from outside the house. He had collected food from almost all the houses in the street. Three quarters of his pot was full by now. Since it was the house at the end of the street, it stood outside the reach of the street light. Darkness grimly engulfed that corner of the street. It must be past nine: the street was quiet, without the usual noise of its inhabitants. He was anxious about how hungry his family must be by now. He was more worried about keeping his grandson waiting for food. He wondered what tantrum the hungry child must be throwing at home now. He would weep until his face looked swollen. Maasaanam wanted to get home quickly. His home was just one kilometer away from here. He would have to go past the houses of the upper caste and then cross the road. It was a straightforward route.

"*Emmov*..."

Maasaanam called out again. He was anxious to go home soon.

Mookkammal came to the door with her child in her arms. She must have been struggling in the kitchen: she was sweating profusely. Holding her child in her left arm, she pulled the end of her saree in her right hand and wiped her face. The baby in her arm was bawling aloud, tears and snot flowing down. The baby's cry shattered the silence of the street.

"The blasted stove... it refuses to get lit up... And this little devil is not shutting up either! *Saniyan*"

She landed a sharp slap on the child's back. The baby bawled out louder than before.

"Why is it crying, *ma*?" Maasaanam asked.

"Why else would it cry? It's hungry… As if I'm starving it deliberately while I have a potful of rice stored!"

"Where is the father, *ma*?"

"He's gone to the landlord's house… Went a long time ago… Not back yet… Not sure what work the landlord has given him!"

The landlord's house was just a short walk away from there. Mookkammal and her husband have been weeding the landlord's chilli field, and the husband had now gone to the landlord's to collect their wages. He had left only in the dusk; the landlord must have sent him on an urgent errand. Mookkammal guessed that was the reason her husband was not home yet.

"Make some porridge from leftovers and feed it, *ma*?"

"Easy for you to say! I just got home and lit up the stove… As if we are royalty to have excess food lying around! Talking like a fool…" she chided Maasaanam light-heartedly.

"Leave the baby here and go, *ma*. See how it stops crying."

"Here, put some of that powder in this *saniyan*'s eyes… Let's see if it stops weeping at least then… Insolent little thing!"

Mookkammal placed the baby hard on the cow-dung-smeared floor and went inside the house. It was a thatched house with a low lintel. She had to duck when she went inside. She was anxious to finish cooking before her husband returned. How he had stood in the hot sun weeding in the middle of the chilli field all day!

The jasmine-like rice frothed and boiled. Mookkammal put a ladle in the pot, scooped some rice and tested its consistency. She knew that she could let it boil a little longer.

After letting it boil more, she drained the water and took the pot off the stove. Once the steam had escaped, she took a couple of scoops of rice on a plate and came out in a hurry.

It struck her only now. The fact that the baby had gone quiet after she had handed it over to Maasaanam dawned on her. What had silenced the child? What had Maasaanam done?

What she saw in the dark entrance of the house appalled her. Her body shuddered. Her face contorted in revulsion.

Cradling the baby on his lap, Maasaanam was scooping food from his pot in small quantities and feeding the baby. The hungry baby was eagerly swallowing the food; its appetite satiated, the baby had stopped crying.

Mookkammal exploded. Leaving the plate with rice on the floor, she hurried towards Maasaanam. She plucked the baby from him. Her lips trembled in anger.

"What have you done! Such a foolish thing… My child has not stooped so low as to have *oorchoru*… Don't dare to do things like this. Do you understand?"

"Is it wrong to feed a hungry child, *ma*?"

"Oh, he dares to speak after what he's done! Talking of right and wrong…"

Mookkammal scowled at Maasaanam. Her glare turned towards the baby. It started crying as its food had been taken away.

"*Saniyan*... All because of this thing! Die, you, little devil!"

Two stinging slaps fell on the child's back. Maasaanam understood that the slaps were meant for him. Downcast, he got up and took his pot.

"Don't hit the baby... Innocent thing... what does it know?"

He walked away from the house. A dejected walk. It looked like he was lost in thought.

Mookkammal realized that Maasaanam was leaving without collecting the food she had brought on the plate. She wondered if he had forgotten about it in the fuss she had made. She wanted to call out to him and give him the food, but hesitated.

Only Maasaanam knew that he had not forgotten it.

Glossary

oorchoru - food collected from all houses in the village in return for one's services

A RARE FLOWER

P SIVAKAMI

I had thought I would be able to sleep at least after dawn. But it was not to be. Sleeplessness had brought on a headache. Narmada would arrive at eight on the dot. I must get ready before that.

The heat of summer has waned and the rainy season has begun. You can imagine what that means in a place like Shimoga. Right from June, the Sahayadri mountain range that traverses Theerthahalli and Soraba blocks the path of the rain clouds and wrings the rain out of them. Last year, in the rainy season, the sea at Bhatkal overflowed its backwaters and dumped a flood on the city!

Let me at least have a stroll in the morning, I thought. I went out into the garden. The change of season often brings cholera and all sorts of infections. I had caught a heavy cold. The moment I stepped into the garden I started sneezing uncontrollably. On top of that, a few tiny black

---

Translated by Malini Seshadri
Original Source: Ariya Malar, *Dalit Sirukathai Thoguppu:* An Anthology of Dalit Short Stories compiled by P Sivakami (Sahitya Akademi, 2014)

insects that had come out after the showers got into my nostrils. Gulmohar flowers, sodden in the overnight rain lay mashed underfoot. These are the rainy season memories I have stored away in my mind.

I travel a fair bit, but I always try to ensure that I'm not away from home for more than three days at a time. This trip, however, had not been one planned by me. I had to travel away from home for about a month on some important office work. I had to move around a lot to investigate and gather information. Because the purpose of this trip was so important, and also because I could not speak Kannada, the management had deputed an officer called Narmada to accompany me. She held an important post in the district *panchayat* office.

Narmada must have been a beauty in her younger years. Even now her skin had a healthy bloom like a *raspuri* mango fruit. The folds of the sari could not mask the grace of her waist. The sparkle from a single tiny nose-stud illuminated her wide face.

Our relationship was unique. She perennially made me aware of two things: one, that she knew it was her duty to respect me, and two, that she did not feel any respect towards me. Was this my fault or hers? I wasn't a hundred percent sure.

On our journey here, I had opened a book I had brought with me to read. It was a story about Americans, written in English. She asked to look at it. After glancing through it for a bit, she turned to me and said "You are very easy to get along with." She said it in English. Oh, and did you learn that from looking through that book, I wanted to ask. Instead I said, "I am the superior officer only in the workplace. At other times I move with all my colleagues as friends."

"But a majority of people are not like that," she remarked. "Why is that?"

I took this as merely her attempt at flattery. I immersed myself in the book.

"When your fellow-student Thimmappa was working in our office, I was the one he always asked to accompany him on all office trips.

Memories of Thimmappa swirled like thick fog in my mind. Those were the days when he had his eye on a friend of mine. She was an aspiring poet. It turned out that Thimmappa wrote short stories. My poet friend once informed me proudly that she was the real protagonist in Thimmappa's story titled "Those same eyes". It's said that even a clever man's lie will stand exposed within eight days. Well, Thimmappa's lie was exposed the very next day. Someone who happened to read Thimmappa's Kannada story shattered the bubble by proclaiming publicly that this was actually a story published earlier by a famous writer. For good measure, this debunker of Thimmappa's lie also threw in a few tidbits about the fake writer himself. It emerged that Thimmappa was the father of three children, all daughters. And that when he had gone to London for higher studies he had met and married a Filipino woman, completed his studies using her money, and then promptly divorced her and returned to India.

These revelations had stunned my friend the budding poet.

"Thimmappa never takes his wife and children with him on any trips," Narmada remarked. This news was of no interest to me.

She held forth about the famous red chillies of the Bedige region. "They're not pungent, in fact slightly sweet. In addition to giving the food a nice colour, they are also very good for stimulating the appetite."

I assumed that since she had studied Nutrition for her post-graduate degree she liked to talk about foods and their nutrients. But then suddenly, as though offering an explanation, she said, "After all, Brahmins love good food, don't they?"

Even before one crosses the border of Shimoga district, one encounters Shivappa Nayak's palace. An aged white-moustached Shivappa gazes out of a well-preserved photograph. He is clad in a skirt-like *dhoti*, an elaborately embroidered and gold-lace-embellished *kurta* and the usual turban, etc. From a present-day perspective I have often wondered why kings were all dressed like clowns. This Shivappa had usurped and amassed vast quantities of land, even using lethal weapons in the process. As I was examining the palm leaf manuscripts that recorded these violent exploits of Shivappa, Narmada whispered in my ear, "There's a Vishnu temple nearby. I had given them advance notice of our programme, so they are all waiting for us there." In response to my unspoken question she said, "They say it is a very ancient temple," and went on to explain its significance.

At the temple, a bunch of *purohits*, heads half-shaven and sporting *kudumis*, were reciting Sanskrit prayers in loud voices, decorating the idol, nothing but a piece of stone, and playing with it like a child would with a doll. If antiquity bestows divinity, then the Vedas may be said to be divine. But apart from their sheer antiquity, is there anything else of value in the Vedas? Having embarked on this line of thought, questions bubbled up in my mind. Is it possible to be liberated from the illusory aura conferred by antiquity?

When the priest brought around the *deepam* plate with its camphor flame for collecting offerings from the devotees, Narmada flung a generous offering of a hundred rupees on the plate. "That's *tulasi* water," she admonished me, noticing that I was washing my hands instead of sipping it when the priest spooned the water into my hands.

"From now on, let us avoid visits to wayside temples when we are travelling, particularly if there is no artistic merit to them," I suggested.

Narmada decided that I should see a *goshala*, a shelter for cows, which housed a number of attractive cows and bulls. Narmada scored a point with me by explaining that the large native variety of cattle brought from Rajasthan were far superior to any foreign breed of cattle or even cross-breeds. There was a particular bull named Mahanandi, huge and glistening black. His tall hump was gracefully curved. There were also quite a few other breeds of bulls and cows.

Just nearby was a poster. It carried a picture of the junior pontiff of the mutt to which the *goshala* was attached. The pontiff's eyes were as large and wide as those of the cows themselves, and he was gently stroking a calf. Inset in one corner of the poster was the photograph of the local MLA. After all, doesn't every person sing his own praises out of fear of being out of the public eye?

At the front of the *goshala*, tooth powder made from cow urine was on sale. I bought some.

Narmada informed me in a rather apologetic tone, "The head of the *matam* would like to meet you because you are visiting from such a great distance."

We were asked to wait in a large room for a few minutes. Many people had already been waiting outside. I wondered whether they would resent us for having been admitted inside the moment we arrived.

Soon a saffron-clad young man entered, holding a silver-handled *saamaram* and a silver pot and heralded, "Here he comes...here he comes...". Instantly, everyone including Narmada scrambled to their feet. The officer appointed to assist the pontiff was a retired police chief. He had retired from service only two months ago. Narmada drew my attention to this emaciated figure standing in a corner, arms crossed, his sacred thread visible on his bare chest.

A cow wearing tiger skin...a tiger wearing the hide of a cow. Before retirement..after retirement. Equilibrium. My mind was busy with such thoughts.

But why these kinds of thoughts? Why should I not think that after one retires, life should be all about Rama, Krishna and service to God? Either that or about paying attention to securing a means of livelihood. Wasn't that so?

The plump pontiff waddled over to where I was sitting

cross-legged on the floor. The retired police chief introduced me to the pontiff.

"You have come from far away, travelling through dense forests to get to this humble place. Your yoga must be what has brought you here." As the 'retiree' was about to explain the term 'yoga" to me, I stopped him and indicated that I knew what it meant.

The pontiff handed me a silk saree. Dark yellow with red checks and a thin gold lace border. Not being of a mind to accept a free gift like a needy villager, I declined to take it.

"This is given only to a chosen few; it's a special *prasadam*, a holy offering," urged the retired one.

"Please stay and partake of our simple meal," said the pontiff.

"No. We don't have the time."

"At least accept a drink to relieve your thirst."

Ripe rasavali bananas, cow's milk, cashew nuts and raisins were offered to us.

As we came out, I noticed that areca nut plantations covered the two hundred and fifty acres of land around the mutt. Several dark-skinned workers were working on the land.

"It's not acceptable for humans to prostrate in front of other humans," I said, offering my opinion.

"He is our family's guru, and so it is absolutely appropriate for us to do so," replied Narmada firmly. She went on to add assorted snippets of information: "The two thousand acres of land that had once belonged to the mutt had been snatched away. There's no space left for animals any more. Cows are being slaughtered for their meat. Man has no respect for Nature."

As we approached Theerthahalli, the sun was sinking in the western sky behind the areca plantations. The car, utterly oblivious to the fact that my tongue had refrained from tasting the *prasadams*, was moving with agonising slowness up and down the many slopes in the road.

Theerthahalli is just a small village. Past the village, in the middle of the forest, dinner had been arranged for us at a small wayside guest house. We dined on chapathis that were as dry and stiff as *appalams*, along with fried lady's-finger curry that had gone cold.

"Don't people eat beef in this area?" I asked. Narmada, seemingly startled by my question, made an effort to compose herself. The cook who was serving us said, "We don't cook such things in our eatery."

After the meal, I continued to probe for information. It was six in the evening by the time I was done with all my questioning and cross-questioning.

As we approached Shimoga on our return journey, Narmada again started talking about this and that. "Devanagere was famous for its voile sarees. But now the looms have been shut down. The effect of globalisation," she remarked.

"In Tamil Nadu too the handlooms are suffering this same fate," I pointed out.

"I always wear only either silk or cotton. But now the prices of polyester and synthetics have fallen very low. In the office all the peons and clerks are always turned out only in synthetic sarees of various kinds. That's why I switched to wearing only silk or cotton exclusively."

One section of society is status-conscious and eager to establish its superiority at every turn; and there is the other section which aspires to shed all labels and merge into the mainstream as equals. My mind was drawn naturally towards exploring this line of thought.

Recently I visited the home of a Brahmin woman. I was served coffee in a porcelain cup while the Brahmin colleague who had accompanied me received her coffee in a stainless steel tumbler-and-tabara* set. That particular incident was at the top of my mind after listening to Narmada's remarks.

I tossed and turned the whole night. Neither the TV nor the books I had taken along with me could hold my attention. I was also coughing and blowing my nose all the time.

The next morning we set out towards Saagar. As the car travelled though forests filled with wild flowers freshened by rain, I found I could not keep my eyes open. Sleep swept over me. Since my nose was blocked, my mouth had opened in my sleep. The cold blast of air dried my throat further and set off a new wave of coughing.

"You're not well," said Narmada in a sympathetic tone. "When we reach Saagar, shall I send for a doctor?"

"Oh, it's just an ordinary cold. It'll go away on its own, no need for a doctor."

Narmada offered a piece of health advice to my ailing self. She said, "As they grow older, many people switch to a vegetarian diet. A vegetarian diet is the healthiest."

"Well, people say it is best to avoid red meat since it is difficult to digest. But foods like fish, which is easily digestible, or soups made with low-fat meats may be eaten. Are you suggesting that only meat-eating needs to stop as one ages? What about ghee, cream, vegetarian snacks fried in high-fat vanaspati, sugar-laden sweets, and gas-producing vegetables like plantain, potato and cluster beans?

Narmada wordlessly rejected this argument by shaking her head emphatically from side to side. Is this the nutrition science they taught you, I wanted to ask. But I restrained myself.

"The Mookambigai temple at Kollur is quite near by. If you want to, we could visit it on our return journey," said Narmada. I was leaning back with eyes closed. She went on:

"It's said that Adi Shankara himself installed the idol of Mookambigai there. Even today this whole region is covered in thick forests. Back in those days, there would have been no roads, no transport. So he must have walked all the way. It just shows that he must have received special blessings from God," remarked Narmada.

The car stopped next to a school. As part of the Sarva Shiksha Abhiyaan scheme, the schools had been painted in the tricolour of the flag. On the wall were displayed the portraits of seven Kannada language writers who had received the Jnanapith Award. Having checked their names, I mentioned a couple of the books they had written. I also mentioned a bit about Devanuru Mahadeva and Siddhalingayya. Narmada assured me that nobody there would have the slightest clue about those two.

"Seven writers received the Jnanpith; yet only Kuvempu is being made much of. So, the author's status has nothing to do with the actual quality of the writing, only with his birth. He won the prize for his Ramayana Darshan. Nothing special about the book. But he belonged to the Vokkaliga caste who are wealthy landowners and the most powerful caste in Karnataka. Of all the seven Jnanpith awardees, he was the only one in whose name the government set up a memorial building, besides gifting a thousand acres of forest land to a trust that bore his name. On top of all this, the government established a university in his name; the Vice-Chancellor was none other than his own son-in-law, Chidananda Gowda. The latter set his father-in-law's tomb between rocky mountain cliffs and named it "Kavishaila". And that's not the whole story... If you have the time we can stop by at his memorial house on the way back."

All these details about Kuvempu were absolute news to me.

Here the Sharavathy river merges into the sea. Even though, many rivers merge into it, the sea never loses its innate quality.

Since the backwaters overflowed and flooded the town, some of the people had been allotted alternative housing on higher ground. Megane was one such location. We were ascending the steep gradient of the mountain. Becoming aware of the scent of *ketaki* flowers, I couldn't resist asking about it. And sure enough we came across them nearby...the tender new yellow leaves of screwpine.

It is a special joy when one's conjectures come true. After all, conjectures play an important role in foretelling future events. Like the scent of screwpine wafting in the air, don't waves of thoughts and ideas also travel around in the ether? Surely they will meet up at some time, somewhere, with a sentient mind? Problems were besetting me from all sides. But I derived some comfort from the thought that I would win through by my own effort.

Once we arrived at Megane, Narmada began to relate a story:

"The Dalits who live here refer to Parusurama's wife Renuka as Renuki Amman. A special puja is conducted for the goddess who is worshipped in her nude form. It's a very ancient tradition. Recently some Dalit groups in Karnataka raised an objection to this practice and carried on an agitation demanding that it be stopped. At the next special puja after the agitation, this area was swarming with people who had come to see the worship of the nude goddess. Very few had heard about the nude goddess till the agitation made news. It's just like the saying we have in Tamil about the passing mendicant ruining a perfectly good conch by picking it up and blowing into it instead of just letting it lie there."

"Is this puja practice still going on?"

"No, the authorities put a stop to it because of the continued agitation by the Dalit groups. But maybe the locals are still carrying it out in secret...."

I detected a note of distaste and disparagement whenever Narmada mentioned 'Dalit groups'. I wondered why.

On our way back, I spotted a rare species of plant, a wild variety that can be found only on hillsides. It has a swollen, bulbous root from which sprouts a smooth stem like a spectacled Russell's viper. At the tip, a tender shoot the colour of a peeled onion and shaped like a *shivalingam*. Encircling that, the flower....a single layer of pale pink petals. With considerable effort our driver was able to get to the plant and pick the flower to oblige me. I put it away carefully.

As we entered the premises of Kuvempu Memorial I noticed automatic sprinklers turned on at full blast to water the three sprawling acres of lawn. A tile-roofed, two-storeyed old mansion. Even larger than Shivappa Nayak's palace. This is his ancestral property. At the rear stands a fifty-acre flourishing areca nut plantation. That too is part of the property!

An exquisite teak-carved palanquin, extensive horse stables, a large bathing chamber with hot water laid on—all these stood proud testimony to the glory of his ancestors. Inside the building, soothing Carnatic music caressed the visitors' ears. It took about half an hour to complete the tour of Kuvempu's bedroom, study, and so on. In the Kuvempu museum, all manner of memorabilia from sandals to a sample of his hair were carefully preserved. A multitude of photographs recorded his life events from birth to death. Even the incident that took place in his final days was on record—the one where he had been brought here from Mysore by helicopter at the government's expense. He had been Vice-Chancellor of Mysore University. Now his son Poorna Chandra Tejasvi is a Professor at that same university. Phrases from Kuvempu's poems accompanied the photographs of birds that his son had captured on camera.

A stone's throw from the Kuvempu mansion was Kavishaila. Here granite slabs had been artistically arranged in a contemporary design. Narmada informed me,

"Whenever he felt the urge to write he would come to this spot and turn his gaze on the wide expanse of forest. This is where the Ramayana Darshanam [the award winning book by Kuvempu] took shape." In this manner, stories and rumours about Kuvempu were being tossed at me by Narmada. I could detect an underlying contemptuous tone in her commentary.

An elephant, dead or alive, is worth a thousand sovereigns of gold, says a proverb. But elephant... or cat...which one is this, I couldn't help speculating. An uncharitable thought, really, because I hadn't actually read Kuvempu's work.

When we got back to Shimoga, Kittaan was there to receive me. He is also an officer, like me. He was wearing shorts and a banian in readiness for his stroll. After getting acquainted over the customary cup of tea, I went into my room.

I was with Narmada discussing the preparation of the investigation report on the matters that had arisen during the day, and planning the next day's schedule of work. She remarked, "Kittaan reminds me of my former boss. Did you know, Kittaan shirks work. The office staff say he regularly takes off for Bangalore by car for drinking sessions with his friends. My former boss was an SC. And a cinema actor on top of that. How can you be an officer and also act in movies? How are lady officers like me expected to take files to him for signature? Such indecent behaviour! In fact he was sort of indecent even to look at. Once when I went to him to get his signature on a file I saw that he had rubbed oil all over his body...like a rowdy."

"Well, even in my State, former film actors and even

current film actors are occupying posts from Chief Minister to people's representatives. Aren't we all staying mute and docile about it? Isn't this going on all over India? No one seems to think that being a film actor is a disqualification."

"That's not it, Ma'am. Let him act in films. But he was so indecent in appearance...I don't know how to describe it...."

This affliction that made her boss distasteful in Narmada's eyes, and which she claimed she was unable to describe...what was it? It wasn't just that he was a film actor, or even that his behaviour lacked culture, it was mainly because of his backward caste. This was the true nature of his affliction.

Narmada handed me some pills that she had got for me from a doctor. She wished me a quick recovery from my cold, and left the room.

When I said I wanted nothing more than a banana and a glass of milk for dinner, the man on kitchen duty offered to make hot pepper soup for me. Even as he was speaking, the phlegm in his congested lungs made its presence felt. I had half a mind to urge him to look after his health. But then I wondered how long this disease had lived within that wiry frame. I said nothing.

As I was sipping the hot soup and trying to clear my cold through eyes and nose, there was a knock at the door. "I heard you were not well", said Kittaan as he entered, in a tone of concern.

"After all, you are my senior officer. So if I don't make enquiries about your health, that itself would become a talking point, right?" he asked lightly.

I responded in a similar tone, "Being a senior officer isn't some sin or something. It's just that I have become older, that's all."

"No, no. I'm sure you're younger than me." And he went on to inform me that he was fifty two.

We chatted about this and that for a while. He was describing the extreme poverty and illiteracy in his home state in the North-east of the country.

"I miss eating pork," he said, "the thought of it makes my mouth water."

And then: "You seem to work very hard?" I did not respond. He went on: "This is the seventh time I've been assigned this kind of posting, one that no one else wants. They have been shunting me to these errand boy kinds of jobs like some wandering mendicant. So I am just not going to do any work. That's it. I like to roam around like this. That way I can get away from my problems with my wife, right? Yet, my wife doesn't allow me even this limited freedom. She harasses me by calling me very often on my cellphone."

Even before he could finish the sentence, his cellphone rang. Must be she again, he said, before proceeding to answer the call. When the call was over, he said, "It's about some trifling thing...not worth mentioning. Do you know how she starts off the topic? We earn our money the hard way by sweat and toil, don't we? I respond, yes. Then how could the woman who lives next door steal four days' worth of our dog food? What could I say to that? Okay, okay, I will talk later, I said, and cut her off." *Adaada*....women...!

This led us to an enjoyable exchange of anecdotes about our respective pets.

"It's a good idea to present a puppy as a wedding gift. Whether the marriage survives or not, it's certain that the dog's affection will last."

In time, the topic returned to office matters and officers.

"When the junior officers see their seniors toeing the politicians' line, they also fall into the groove," commented Kittaan, as a preliminary to something else he wanted to say.

"If the mother tigress jumps eight feet, the cub will jump sixteen feet.....that's how the saying goes, right?" I remarked.

"They all thought I was Bansi Lal*'s man. Then when Om Prakash Chauthala came they said I'm Chauthala's man. As for my wife, she claims I'm her man. But alas, in this situation, I'm nobody's man. I'm just an orphan."

I laughed.

"Aha, you actually laughed aloud. You've broken the 'boss barrier' between us."

I laughed some more.

"That was during my training period. My boss, poor fellow, was a workaholic. He was immersed in work from six in the morning till eight at night. But very feudal. One part of his house was a kind of informal office. You know how it goes. Once, on a holiday, he sent his *chaprasi** (which in this case means an office employee, of course) to fetch me to his home office. He could just have called me over the telephone, right? I rushed there thinking it was some kind of emergency. He made me just sit there in front of him while he talked with someone on the phone. They talked and talked. On and on. Next he opened some files and started studying them. I sat there for an hour in front of him with no clue about why I had been summoned. Then the intercom buzzed. He answered it and rose to leave the room. Since I had to show respect to my boss, I also stood up. In a short while he returned. I stood up again. Another summons on the intercom; he got up to leave; this time I stayed seated. In a few minutes he was back. I stayed in my chair. He noticed this and said in Hindi: 'Jab senior officer aathe hain, udtha kartha hai.' Meaning, when a senior officer arrives one is expected to stand. "I was seething with anger. But I sat with my head bowed and said nothing. When the third summons came and he left once more, I not only stayed seated but also took out a cigarette and started smoking. He returned to the room when I was half way through my cigarette. I continued to smoke it to the end and then stubbed it out. Just because his wife summons him a hundred times from inside, am I supposed to jump up and down every time the rascal leaves the room and returns?" Kittaan apologised for using a swear word and then continued his story.

"Do you know what he does next? He tells me, 'Kittaan, don't come anywhere near me again. You don't need any training. Don't worry that I will write a negative report about you.' After that day, I avoided him totally. But he kept his word. I'm telling you all this because I'm trying to point out that it's important for bosses to be pleasant and friendly. I don't like it when those who have joined just two or three years later are being treated like *chaprasis.*"

I asked Kittaan, "In what way should *chaprasis* be treated?" He laughed and replied, "Well, *chaprasis* should be treated like *chaprasis.*" "I'm joking," he added.

"Actually, that boss was at least honest unlike a lot of others. But his sense of self-righteousness made him arrogant. He assumed that everyone except himself was a crook. He was close to the Chief Minister.

I interrupted to remark, "That's surprising!"

"Why should it be surprising? It's convenient to keep an honest officer close to you, one who won't take bribes. Then the entire earnings will fall directly into your kitty instead of leaking or having to be shared. And the officer will also be happy that his honesty has been recognised."

"Oh, okay, go on."

"I went to meet this officer on a personal matter. He is a Brahmin SC."

"I don't understand."

"He is an SC who behaves as if he's a Brahmin. Listen to this. As soon as I entered he looked at me as if I was a cow or goat that had strayed in. While shaking hands, some people just go through the motions, offering a hand that feels like a dead fish. This man wasn't prepared to do even that. "What's it, Kittaan, what's the matter?" he asked in a supercilious tone. I said, "Er....nothing." I just walked past him, shook hands with another officer who had come to meet him and whom I knew, and went away."

I had been listening patiently to his story. Now I asked

mildly, "So tribal people from the North Eastern states aren't given important posts in your State?"

"No, no, nothing like that. It all depends on how one behaves. Only the fellow who holds out his hand for bribes and the fellow who salutes his boss survive and thrive. I can't ever do those things. I am speaking to you frankly. I just want to carry on peacefully without complications of any kind. I don't like to slog all hours or compete with anyone to prove who can work more. So I am content with where I am now."

I did not say anything.

"Have you been to Manipur?" he asked.

"No."

"That is my home district. To this day the people there are illiterate and have no basic amenities. The MLA who won the election from my district is illiterate himself. He had never even visited a city. When he came to the capital, he noticed that people were talking on telephones. He wanted to convey a message to his friend back home in the village. So what does he do? He goes and picks up a telephone receiver and starts talking into it without dialling any number. 'I will be returning tomorrow,'he says into the phone, 'and I will meet you then.' Then he replaces the receiver, and he's done! When the people around wanted to know whom he had talked to, he said he had talked to his friend. Does your friend have a telephone, what's his number, they asked. He gaped uncomprehendingly as though dumbstruck with fright. So then somebody had to explain to him how the telephone works. I am from that backward district myself.

So what I am now is good enough for me."

Kittaan was capable of going on and on like this for hours if he was allowed to. But I had to get my report written. So I politely expressed my regrets to him, showed him out and shut and bolted the door.

It was midnight by the time I finished the report. As I switched off the light and fell onto my bed, the thought came into my head: where is that special, rare flower?

Glossary

Panchayat : Village council
Raspuri: A variety of mango fruit
Bedige: Alternatively, Byadgi, a district in Karnataka
Dhoti: Traditional wrap-around lower garment for men
Kurta: Loose-fitting long upper garment
Purohit: Temple priest
Kudumi: Tuft of hair worn traditionally by priests
Deepam: Lamp
Tulasi: Plant whose leaves are used in worship
Matam: A Hindu religious institution
Saamaaram: Ceremonial hand-held fan

Prasadam: Food offered to the Lord, distributed to devotees
Appalams: Thin circles of soaked and ground rice or lentils, dried in the sun and roasted or fried as a side dish
Tumbler-and-Tabara: Set of two utensils for pouring out and drinking beverages
Mookambikai: A form of Goddess Parvathi
Adi Shankara: Eighth Century Indian philosopher and theologian
Sarva Shiksha Abhiyaan: Government of India's programme to universalize primary education
Jnanpith Award: Oldest and most prestigious Indian annual award for literature
Shivalingam: Stone represenatation of Lord Siva in temples
Bansilal: Former Chief Minister of Haryana
Om Prakash Cahauthala: Former Chief Minister of Haryana
Chaprasi: Peon

THE GOVERNMENT SCHOOL

IMAYAM

"Where is he, *di*?" asked Valli.

"In the next class, *ma*," replied Shalini.

"Come quick."

"Don't shout too much!"

Ignoring her, Valli rushed into the classroom. Shalini stood hesitantly at the door.

Just as Ponnambalam was writing "Rights and Duties of Indian Citizens" on the blackboard, Valli asked, "Why did you throw my daughter out of the class two days in a row?"

"Who are you? Can you just walk into the class? Could you not ask me for permission?" Ponnambalam asked.

"Why have you not been letting my daughter into the class?" Valli repeated, paying no attention to his questions.

He realized who she was only after he saw Shalini standing at the door. "Are you that girl's mother?"

"Yes, yes… Now tell me why. I need to go!"

Translated by V.Ramakrishnan

Original Source:. Arasangha Pallikoodam, 2014, Imayam's anthology 'Saavu Soru'

"Do you know what your daughter did?"

"What, did she commit murder?" Valli raised her voice.

Her attitude and tone irritated him. "Do you know what I asked her to do?" Ponnambalam asked patiently, not letting his irritation show.

"You were the one who threw her out of the class, right?"

"I didn't throw her out. I just asked her to meet the Headmaster."

"In a class of so many students, why should she be the one to meet the Headmaster?" Valli barked.

"Would I send her without reason?"

"Was it you or the Headmaster who asked her to get out of the class?"

"It was me."

"Then why should she meet the Headmaster?"

"Why are you shouting now, *ma*? Is this a classroom or marketplace?" Ponnambalam asked loudly. In the same breath, he shouted at the students: "Mind your studies now. There's nothing here for you to gape at."

Not minding Ponnambalam's raised voice, Valli responded disdainfully: "We know this is a school. If you ask students to meet the Headmaster or bring their parents as you wish, can we appear at your convenience? Don't we have other business? Are we like you, sitting in one place and earning?"

Ponnambalam's face grew taut with anger. "Who do you think sits in one place and earns?" he sputtered.

"Am I the one getting weekends off and vacations every four months? The contractor pays us only if we show up for work. Would we earn anything if we didn't?" she snapped.

Ponnambalam glared at her, lost for words. He looked at Shalini, who was still at the door, and then turned to his class. "Is it nice to make so much noise when people are talking? Study the lesson titled 'Rights and Duties of Citizens as Written in the Indian Constitution.' I'll test you on it," he barked. The silence that followed hardly lasted a minute and gradually dissolved into a babble again.

"I need to go to work, sir. Give me an answer!"

"Please understand what I'm saying. I didn't throw her out. Ask your daughter, I just asked her to meet the Headmaster."

"As a teacher, you could have handled this by yourself. Why ask her to meet the Headmaster? If you send them to the Headmaster for every little thing, he would tell us he can't take care of such disobedient donkeys, kick them out, and hand us the *TC*. He's such a rascal!"

Ponnambalam stood staring at Valli. 'Smart lady, indeed,' he thought to himself, and muttered, "What a mouth!"

"Meeting the Headmaster is not such a big thing. And he won't hand out TCs for every little thing. Don't we have the authority to correct students?" he asked.

"Tell me, what crime did my daughter commit?" Valli asked mockingly. Her loud voice and stubbornness irked him.

Still not betraying his emotions, he said, "She distributed chocolates to all the students in the class to celebrate the birthday of the actor known as 'Tamil Lion.' Can I not tell her it is unbecoming of a student? It's for her own good that

I did it."

"You need not worry about what's good for my daughter. Just do what you are paid for. I have lost the day's wages because of you."

Her words incensed Ponnambalam. He considered reprimanding her and sending her out, but wondered what he would do if she yelled louder. His anger turned on himself. Why did he care what students did? He also wondered why he had accepted this government job.

In his days, since most students selected History, he chose the same major. He did not know then that the job prospects for History graduates were very low. It was only three months ago, at the age of fifty-two, that he had secured this job on account of seniority. He had not anticipated such issues when he started the job. Given that it was a government job, and that too as a teacher, he thought it would be easy. He had not fathomed that anyone could question or scold him, or worse, that women could yell at him so freely. He was furious at Valli for fighting with him instead of scolding her daughter. He could not believe that a woman was tactlessly yelling at him in the middle of a class. She stood there like a rooster ready for a fight.

"Sir, Kamala took my notebook and refuses to give it back," a girl from the class complained to him.

"Off you go! Aren't you old enough not to come whining about such petty things?" he yelled and sent the girl back in tears. He immediately turned to Valli and said, "Am I spoiling your child? You are now fighting with me just because I asked her to meet the Headmaster! How can we chastise students then? How will they listen to us or obey us?"

"So, you would throw a child out of class for two days for a small misconduct?"

"Why do you keep saying I threw her out? I never did."

"Are you telling me she came out of the class on her own?"

"You need to be sensible. Your daughter is not a little child. She's in the twelfth grade. It is out of concern for her that I chastised her."

"We know all about your concern. As if you treat these children like your own! Don't we know what you do, summoning them to the lab, staff room or for tuition? It is all exposed on the TV. I wonder what unspeakable miseries children in lower grades face!"

"Don't talk loosely. There are over three thousand students studying in this school, and all of them are girls. Why, there are over ninety students in your daughter's class. There has not been a single complaint."

"Don't you threaten students with poor scores if they don't attend your private tuitions?"

"I'm not the Science teacher. You need to know who you are talking to," Ponnambalam snapped at her.

"How much longer are you going to keep her out of the class?" Valli spat back.

"A class is going on here. And here you are, unceremoniously entering and yelping at me! Can you enter a private school and talk this way? They would just give you the TC and send your daughter home if you do it."

"Why would we be here if we could afford private

schools?" her voice drowned his.

Ponnambalam's voice grew tired after a few more heated exchanges. He beckoned Shalini over and asked her, "What wrong did I do for you to bring someone from home and unleash them on me? Where did you learn such behaviour?"

Shalini was silent.

"From you, obviously. Students learn things from their teachers," Valli replied hotly.

"You talk so much! Why can't you scold your daughter? She not only distributed chocolates. Pick any of your daughter's notebooks, and you'll find the 'Tamil Lion' actor's picture pasted on it. She has written his name all over her book. Won't you question her?"

With the satisfaction of having produced concrete evidence to shut Valli up, Ponnambalam smiled.

"You think I didn't? I beat her up at home before bringing her here. She has written the name on her notebook, not tattooed it on her body. Children everywhere do these things. You are just overreacting. Do you know what happened when that actor fell sick? Hundreds of men went to Pazhani and shaved their heads, praying for his quick recovery. They showed it on TV last night, didn't you watch?"

Ponnambalam was frustrated. She had a retort for every argument. Knowing there was no reasoning with her, he said with a finality: "*Amma*, this is a classroom. A whole hour is wasted now. Please go and see the Headmaster."

"Are you the only one who has lost time today? What about me? Looks like this day's wages are down the drain!

When there are so many students in your class, what's wrong with you, *di*? *Saniyan*! Look what trouble you've brought me!" grumbling, Valli stepped out of the classroom. Shalini joined her mother.

"What a miserable morning!" Ponnambalam groaned. "Well, have you all studied the lesson? Ready for a test?" he asked the class. No one made a sound. "Take out your books," he said, and a sudden thought struck him: what if Shalini and her mother made outrageous claims against him to the Headmaster? Knowing by now that Valli was capable of it, he was worried. "Keep studying quietly," he ordered his class and hurried to the Headmaster's room.

He was relieved when he saw Shalini and her mother standing outside the Headmaster's room. "The Headmaster is a crazy fellow. He'll speak one way to you and another way when you're not around. He'll have different tones for male and female teachers. *Saniyan*, I'm fated to meet him so early in the day!" muttering under his breath, he entered the Headmaster's room.

"Come in, sir. Please take a seat," the Headmaster greeted Ponnambalam and turned towards the tenth grade student standing in his room. "Why were you absent for a whole week? You will come and go as you wish, and the authorities above me will blame me for your poor results. Why are you quiet? Answer me." He repeated the question in different ways, but could extract no response from her. "You won't utter a word here, but you'll go home, pile up complaints against me and bring a whole battalion to confront me. Isn't that right?" he asked. There was still no response from her.

"Do you think I have no other work? Donkey! Don't you get what I'm saying? Why do you stand there like a dumb buffallo? Will you open your mouth only if I give you the TC?" he yelled. The girl showed no sign of responding even after the threat of TC. This was not the first girl he had threatened with a TC. It was a threat he used on all his students. It had earned him the name TC Ramalingam not only among students and teachers, but also as far as the offices of the Deputy Educational Officer and the Chief Educational Officer. He had not expelled a single student in his ten years as the Headmaster.

"Don't keep standing there and fall in a faint. Then they'll blame me for that. Why didn't you come to school for a week? Tell me now, or go bring your parents." It was only after the Headmaster shouted again that the girl opened her mouth.

"Stomach ache, sir."

"What?"

"Stomach ache."

"What happened?"

The girl did not open her mouth. After a short pause, the Headmaster asked, "Do your parents know?"

"Yes."

"Which hospital did you go to?"

". . ."

"Do you still have it?"

"I'm fine now."

"All right, go to your class now. If you don't come to school after this, you have to bring your parents. Or else,

I'll hand you the TC. Do you follow me?" the Headmaster asked.

The girl nodded, thanked him and left.

"Do you really think this girl had a stomach ache? She's just pretending. These children know what to say to deceive me. Can I ask a girl what kind of stomach ache she had? Won't it be inappropriate? All these women teachers are the same: they send the students to me for every little thing. Why can't they just give them a good scolding and let them into the class again?" the Headmaster said, and drank some water. "I forgot to ask you what you are here for. Tell me, sir, what can I do for you?"

"The girl standing outside distributed chocolates in her class to celebrate the birthday of the actor named 'Tamil Lion.' Not only that, she has written the actor's name on every page of her notebook. She also has his picture pasted on her books. I asked her to meet you, but she has brought her mother instead. That woman entered my classroom and started yelling at me, sir."

"Let them go rot, sir! Why did you take it this far?" the Headmaster asked. Ponnambalam's face became grim. "Come in, *ma*," the Headmaster called Shalini and her mother in.

"What's the matter, *ma*?"

"My daughter is innocent, sir. Goaded by her classmates, she has distributed chocolates in the class. For that, he threw her out of the class," Valli complained. Before she could finish, Ponnambalam interrupted her and said, "I didn't throw her out, sir. I just sent her to meet you and come back."

"Did you distribute chocolates?" asked the Headmaster.

Shalini did not open her mouth. Instead, her mother said, "Her classmates make her do such things, and she ends up getting into trouble."

"Have you written a movie actor's name all over your notebook?"

". . ."

"Do you have the picture of the actor in your books?"

Shalini didn't look like she was ever going to answer. She stood there as if she was the most obedient student in the school.

"It is fine if you distribute sweets on your birthday. You may even do it on the birthday of your parents or siblings. But does it seem right to give chocolates on a movie actor's birthday?"

"This is exactly what I asked her, sir," Ponnambalam interjected.

"What's wrong with distributing chocolates? She didn't steal the money for it. It was her money. Also, she gave it only to her classmates. I don't understand why you people are discussing this for two days and making a fuss instead of brushing it aside," Valli said.

Masking his anger with a smile, the Headmaster said in a firm voice, "Your daughter is well within her rights to spend her money as she sees fit, I don't deny it. I don't care whose birthdays you celebrate either. Do it on the streets or at home. If you do it at school, then I have a duty to question it. That's what the government pays us for. The HM is not a cop to be afraid of. There's nothing wrong with meeting the HM."

"But how responsible is it to throw a girl of her age out of the class?"

"How many times do I have to tell you that I didn't throw her out? I just sent her to meet the HM and come back," said Ponnambalam. Valli stood her ground as if she had not heard him. Surprised by her bold and unapologetic attitude, the Headmaster's shoulders slumped.

"All right, we shouldn't have asked her why she was celebrating a movie star's birthday. We won't ask her anything at all, is that fine?" the tired Headmaster conceded and took a sip of water. Suddenly, as if a new thought had struck him, he said, "Earlier, parents used to ask teachers to not spare an inch of the students' flesh except the eyes. But now they ask us why we hit them. People threaten us saying, 'Do you know that there are laws that can land teachers in jail if they lay hands on students? You can't hit students as they did earlier, you know? If you don't, you better know now!' When just a verbal enquiry is met with so much resistance these days, how can we even imagine physical punishment?" He seemed to be talking to himself.

Paying no attention to this, Valli said bitterly, "It is because she was thrown out that my daughter returned home the past two days without attending classes. That is why I've had to come here today."

"What's wrong with coming to school, *ma*?"

"Half a day has gone in this ordeal. How can I go to work now? Who will let me work today after this hour? The contractor would make a huge scene about punctuality even if we go to work at nine in the morning," Valli grumbled.

"Where are you from, *ma*?"

"Kazhudhur. If I board the bus at seven, I will reach Viruthachalam by eight. Then, I have to walk from Palakkarai to that day's job site, and it is nine by the time I get there. That, according to them, is late! Tell me how I can go to work today. I go home after work only by eight or nine in the evening, after which I have to make dinner, eat, and go to bed. I can make it to Viruthachalam-Palakkarai on time only if I wake up when the rooster calls. How do you expect parents to come whenever you summon us when our lives are so hectic? Who will pay my wages today, sir?" Valli asked tearfully. The Headmaster's attitude changed once he saw she was close to tears. He looked at the frayed lunch basket that she held in her arm.

"What you say is right, *ma*. We shouldn't question the students, nor can we hit them. You say we can't summon parents either. What other option do we have? Can I tell the Education Officers what you've told me here? Parents pay lakhs at private schools and stand in a queue obediently. Those institutions are merely private tuitions. Parents of students in government schools are mostly like you. We can talk neither to students nor to parents. If we persist in our methods, we are threatened with petitions." The Headmaster's mobile phone rang as he was speaking. Cursing under his breath, he answered. "Hello?"

"What, a meeting? At the CEO's office? When? You need statistics of students by their grade and caste? But I presented it in the last meeting, didn't I? You lost it? Three copies, all right. You don't need any other statistics? All right, I'll be there. I'll also inform other HMs, sir," he said, slapping his forehead in frustration. "How many times do I present the same thing? If they keep calling me for meetings every day, how do I run the school? How do I take classes? How do I produce results? The clerk has chosen a great time to take some time off today! It's not as if he'll do his work if he were here… With excuses of going to the Treasury or the bank, he'll find sanctuary in the tea shop outside. If I question him, he'll threaten me with false accusations of swindling," the Headmaster grumbled. "Can you please bring the peon, sir?" he asked Ponnambalam.

As Ponnambalam left the room, another teacher entered the room with a tearful girl.

"What happened, ma'am?" the Headmaster asked anxiously.

"She has 'attained her age', sir. Shall I send her home?"

"Do you have to come to me for these things? Please go ahead and send her home," he said. But immediately, he called, "Wait, call her parents and ask them to take her home. Let's not send her home alone in this state."

"Where do I keep her until then, sir?"

"On my head," he yelled. The shocked teacher stood waiting for his instructions. "Go, keep her in the staff room. Don't take her back to class, it'll be uncomfortable for her."

The teacher left with the girl.

The Headmaster's frustration found an outlet in Valli now: "See what kinds of problems I deal with every day? Just as you have your troubles, we have ours. And everyone wants to palm their troubles off to someone else," he proceeded to curse the teachers. Having released his feelings, he picked the water bottle and took a few gulps.

"Sir," Valli called him hesitantly.

"You've come here to pick a fight with us just because your daughter was asked to meet me. The teacher you fought with today is the only dedicated fellow here. If a few more parents like you accost him, how can he concentrate on his work?"

"I didn't come to pick a fight, sir. What if she makes some drastic decision because she was thrown out of the class?" Tears were now flowing down her cheeks. "Our lives rely on our daily wages, sir."

"If so, where did she get the money to buy chocolates for the whole class? Do you think a child from a wealthy family would do such things?"

"Children are all the same nowadays, sir, be it a boy or girl. We feel anxious even to confront them!"

"If parents are so afraid of their own children, what can teachers do? That's why all the teachers redirect children to me! Do you understand?"

Valli stood silently.

"Some boy had given a bottle of beer to a twelfth grade girl on Valentine's Day last week. That idiot, without refusing such inappropriate advances, has brought it to school in a Pepsi bottle. She shared the beer with five of her friends when teachers were not around. The news somehow reached a teacher, and the girl was asked about it. That's all. The girl went up to the fourth floor and threatened to jump from there. The other four girls went into a lab and locked themselves in. I promised them that I wouldn't suspend them or summon their parents. Eighty teachers stood around, trying to placate the girl on the fourth floor. Three-thousand children stood watching the spectacle! The girl went up at two in the afternoon and didn't come down until four. Had she jumped, I would've lost my job! I made a thousand promises to persuade her. The silly girl who didn't want the incident to reach her parents' ears made a huge publicity of it herself. When three-thousand students know something, news travels rapidly to every village around here. The teachers and I had a tough time that day until we got all the five girls safely to their respective homes. The poor teacher who asked the girl about the beer was trembling with fear, apologizing to her over and over. A thousand issues like this every day. We look forward to the end of the day even as we begin every day. It feels like we're sitting on fire all the time." The Headmaster paused and looked at the mother and daughter. Shalini stood there like an innocent child. "Did you or did you not see that girl threaten to jump from the fourth floor the other day?"

Shalini nodded.

The Headmaster continued in a tone of delivering a lecture: "At least ten students come here every day, distributing chocolates for their birthday. I take what they give and wish them heartily. Do you see me questioning them all? Wealthy kids spend money blindly without realizing its value. And these kids are tempted to do the same. It's not just kids... Even grown-ups celebrate everything from birthdays to weddings. Did you watch the news yesterday?"

"Where do I have time for all that, sir? If I leave home at seven in the morning, I return only by nine in the evening," Valli said. "These teachers shouldn't be given an audience; they immediately start lecturing!" she mumbled.

"A lady killed herself because her husband did not buy her a new saree for their wedding anniversary. They have a three-month-old infant. It's only been two years since they married. Do we need practices that lead us to such ends? Private schools are basically sophisticated tuition centres that help students attain good scores. People flock there with money only for that. Are you in a state to afford such things?"

Valli did not open her mouth. Beckoning Shalini to his desk, he said, "You're going to be here for only four or five months. Then you won't have to face these teachers anymore. Why don't you listen to them and be good? What's the worst that could happen?"

Ponnambalam entered the room with the peon.

"I took some statistics to the meeting with the Chief Educational Officer last week. Do you know where to find a copy of that? If not, call the clerk and find it."

"I'll check if it's on his table, sir," the peon said and went into the next room.

"If this thing born to me was any good, why would I be standing here now! Neither I nor my parents know what star I was born under. When all the others are all right, why does she have to distribute chocolates?" Valli cried.

"It's all right, *ma.* Please go home." Turning to Shalini,

he said, “You can go to your class now.”

“If only you were obedient… When there are so many quiet students in your class, what’s your problem? My day’s wages are gone!” Chiding Shalini, Valli left the room.

Gesturing to Ponnambalam to take a seat, the Headmaster spoke as though explaining a difficult concept to a child. “Those who come here don’t come for studies. They come here just to kill time. Who would study if everything is given to them for free? The fact that we celebrate birthdays and wedding anniversaries shows that the British have not left our country yet. And worst of all, our country is in the hands of movie actors now! Then why would people not celebrate their birthdays?! Why should we care what they do? Just come to school, do your job, and go home. Even if you don’t do your job, at least try not to bring trouble to me. Even bulls without horns can attack these days,” the Headmaster smiled.

“I have class, sir. Let me go now.” Ponnambalam left.

“All right!” The Headmaster turned towards the peon and asked, “Did you ring the bell for recess?”

A girl entered his room.

“What is it?” the Headmaster asked.

“Teacher asked me to meet you, sir!”

Glossary

TC - Transfer Certificate, a certificate that denotes that a student does not belong to that particular school anymore

THE SWEETEST FRUIT

THEYNMOZHI

The moon had spread silver all over the ground. The central *koodam* of the house and one of the two rooms that led off from it were bathed in moonlight. The coconut fronds outside the window drew sharp shadow-lines across the moonbeams. In the coolness of the house, light and shade were performing an intricate night-dance.

The snake had coiled itself around the window bars and was waving its raised head gently to and fro. The shadow of its wide hood fell alternately upon wall and floor. It was as if the moon shone only for this snake, as if the coconut fronds danced only for this snake. And, oblivious of all else, the snake swayed its hood only for them both.

I was reluctant to tell Appa that I had spotted a snake. He would immediately beat it to death. On the other hand I was afraid of the snake and so I couldn't just keep quiet about it. From the *koodam*, I softly called out to my father.

Translated by Malini Seshadri
Original Source: Theempazham, 2011, Manarkeni journal

Even my muted tone must have carried enough of a hint of urgency to alert him. Amma and *Aatha* were asleep. Appa walked silently towards me and asked what had happened. Wordlessly I pointed at the window. Even though I was not all that terrified of snakes, my outstretched arm was rigid with tension. Seemingly oblivious to all these happenings, the snake continued to sway gently in the moonlight. Appa kept a stout rod in the house for the specific purpose of killing snakes. He went to fetch it and I stayed right there. When he came back with the rod, the snake had disappeared.

This was not the first time such a thing had occurred. Many snake visitors to our house have escaped Appa's attempts to kill them. Snakes seemed to have a particular affinity for our house and they continued to arrive in a steady stream. Not surprising at all because open fields flanked the house on both sides and a wide irrigation channel ran just behind our backyard. The backyard itself was a tangle of bushes and creepers of all kinds, with many plants in front of the house as well. My *Aatha* had heard somewhere that *siriyanangai* and *periyanangai* plants would keep snakes away, and so she had these planted at intervals around the house. Yet several times I myself have seen snakes actually coiled in comfort under those very plants. Also, the brick piles here and there, mounds of rubble and stacks of firewood were like invitations to the snakes and became cosy homes for them.

The moment I realised that the snake was no longer coiled around the window bars, I hurried towards my cupboard and looked at the old book bag I had kept there.

Even in the swirling darkness I could make out wriggling movements inside the bag. The wise snake was there! Some months earlier, when I had opened the cupboard door for something, I had caught the snake by surprise and it hurriedly withdrew its head into the book bag. But not before I had sensed the intense tenderness and love in its eyes.It brought its head out again and seemed to tell me 'I am not a danger to you.'

I ran outside, plucked a handful of jasmine flowers and came back to stand in front of the open cupboard. From the bag, the snake put out a tiny part of its head and its forked tongue and asked for the flowers.

It was really no surprise that I had not felt the least twinge of fear up to that point. I enjoyed its gentle movements. More than that, I loved the thought that it had chosen my cupboard, my book bag to make a home for itself, like some lost sparrow that had somehow landed up in my care. By making no effort to run away on spotting me it won my affection and left no room for revulsion or alarm.

It never left its home in the cupboard. Whenever I visited, it would put out its head and wave its forked tongue at me as though to win me over with its charm. It always behaved the way a loyal friend should. It wept when it told me how its natural defence, its fangs, had been cut away. Like a pleading, innocent child it said it had never bitten anyone. It was always stayed there in that same spot for me. It never moved away.

On the many occasions when Amma cleaned out my cupboard, including my old book bag, she never reported seeing a snake. In fact no one who opened the cupboard ever found a snake there.

Amma looked upon snakes as the messengers of Vanathu Chinnappar. Despite being Hindus, her ancestral family had always, throughout the generations, prayed to the Christians' minor deity Vanathu Chinnappar, and so Amma staunchly believed that snakes would never harm us. Not a day went by without Amma offering a prayer to the picture of Chinnappar. Deep in a forest he stood, one leg slightly bent. A small white cloth wrapped his middle, and he held a spear. His face was resplendent and alive, and there was something princely about his form as he leaned back casually against a tree, with dense bushes and creepers surrounding him. I thought he bore a strong resemblance to the deity Murugan. Amma was known to hold conversations with snakes, and claimed, with some degree of pride, that she could make them obey her and submit to her wishes. Every year she would prepare a rooster as an offering at the snake's nest under a particular mulberry tree in the tamarind grove.

Appa would regularly batter snakes to death and fling their bodies into the fields. Amma would hurry to their resting place with milk and rice to offer as expiation, and pray for forgiveness. The fact that no snake had ever harmed us yet was never pointed out by Amma openly, lest such a statement could attract the evil eye. Instead she would whisper privately, "Snakes are not like people. Snakes always keep their promises." I implicitly believed her claim that she invariably spotted snakes every Tuesday and Friday.

Appa was the direct opposite of Amma when it came

to his approach to snakes. He was intent on killing them at the first available opportunity, and had stored a couple of stout sticks for this express purpose. He never aimed for the head, but always for the middle of the body. And he hardly ever missed. The blow would crush the snake's backbone and cripple it. As it lay unmoving, Appa would pick it up at the end of the stick. Even in that dire situation, the snake would spread its hood and hiss threateningly. Appa would call me to stand beside him to watch. He would wave a stick in front of the hissing snake. It would swoop on the stick and clamp it hard between its jaws, refusing to let go even when the stick was raised high into the air. Amma would scream in indignation. "Why do you bring this burden of sin upon us? Can't you just say you killed it by mistake and toss it away?"

It once happened that Appa and I were standing and talking when I saw a snake crawling across the fence from our neighbour's backyard into ours.Appa was animatedly explaining to me the lyrics of the famous poem '*Engirindhovandaan..*', meaning, 'He came out of nowhere', and expounding on '*Paanayilthelirundhu..*' (the scorpion in the mud pot). Appa was a great admirer of the poet Subramania Bharathi's writings and had internalised most of them. As he described the agony of the Sevagan, the servant persona adopted by Lord Krishna, Appa's face mirrored all the emotions of the character.

Like a snake in thrall to the spell of a snake-charmer's waving flute, I too was reluctant to disrupt Appa when he was in full flow on the topic of Bharathi. I hesitated to mention the snake I had just spotted. I knew that the moment I mentioned it Appa would scurry away to make preparations to finish it off.

Appa viewed snake-killing as a service he was performing by ridding the earth of those devilish creatures. My hesitation was in vain. Appa had noticed that an expression of astonishment had appeared in my eyes that had hitherto been mesmerised by the doings of Sevagan in the Bharathi poem. Yes, I was astonished because that was the longest snake I had ever seen. By this time, the snake had climbed into the rain tree which was even taller than the bamboo plants around it.

'What's the matter, ma?' asked Appa. I pointed to the snake. Appa went up to the foot of the tree and started hurling stones in the direction of the snake. It raised its head a little and leaped from branch to branch. It was like watching a choreographed dance. A small cluster of people of all ages gathered to watch. Some of them commented that, judging from the way the snake was lifting its head, it could well be a cobra. Judging by the speed of its movements, Appa said it could not be a cobra. Some of us youngsters, awed by the sheer length of it, decided it must be a python.

Some of the people tried to shake the tree, some threw stones into the branches, and still others flung rope ends upwards into the tree to wrap around the branches so as to shake them. The snake settled itself on the very tip of the highest branch and basked in the warm sunlight. It had sensed that this spot spelt security for it. The onlookers started tiring one by one and went away. Amma and some of the girls pleaded, 'Please don't kill it, please let it go.' The stand-off continued. Amma also grew tired and went indoors. The snake, finally wearied from this long siege in the midday heat, lost its grip on the branch and fell to the ground. Appa, who had been waiting for this to happen, pounced upon it and finished it off with one massive blow.

Alerted by the noise, everyone rushed out again. Appa took me to where the snake lay dead. I recognized it as a bronze-back snake, which is not venomous.

I rushed to my cupboard and investigated my book bag. The snake was in deep slumber inside. It was in a state of utter exhaustion, as if it had run a marathon, and its deep, dragging breaths could be heard all over the house. I thought it looked very thirsty. I went to fetch a tumbler of water. Appa intercepted me on my way back. 'Where are you taking the water?' he wanted to know. It was as if the house itself was shrinking and expanding with every laboured breath that the snake took. I was worried that Appa would hear the sound of the snake's breaths. But Appa heard nothing. In fact, no one else heard anything.

We youngsters were familiar with a story about bronze-back snakes, and that afternoon we discussed it. As soon as it has bitten someone, a bronze-back snakewill slither away to the cremation ground and wait there. When the snake-bite victim dies and his body is brought for cremation, the snake will hold vigil till the body turns into ashes. Only thereafter will it spit out venom. If the body has not been burnt at the time the venom is spit out, the victim will be restored to life. So if a log or the thick stem of a banana plant were to be burnt on the pyre instead, the lurking snake would be fooled into thinking the victim had been cremated. It would spit out its venom and the victim would get his life back. All this we youngsters implicitly believed as if they were proven facts. This tale about the habits of the bronze-back snake is still very much part of village lore.

Appa had an adversarial relationship with snakes. He would often talk of an occurrence that had made him shed his fear of snakes. When he was a college student, he had once run short of money to pay the exam fee. He had been earning some money by doing day labour in the fields in his spare time to supplement the cost of his studies. It was the height of summer and the fields lay parched in the blazing heat. There was no work for anyone except rat-catchers in those fields. Since rats were pests that ate up the grain, the owner of each field would pay out an agreed amount for every rat caught and killed. Rat-catching was a skill that came naturally to Appa. He liked rat curry too. And there was always some money to be earned by selling the rats he had caught. Appa and his friend went to the fields.

Rat tunnels have two entrances. Appa was always able to spot them quickly.The plan worked like this. While one person spread a thin cloth over one of the tunnel entrances and placed his cupped hands on either side in readiness, the other would take a spade and dig up the other entrance. When the fleeing rat came rushing upwards and pushed against the cloth, it was essential to grab it tightly so that it couldn't escape from its cloth trap.

That day, Appa felt a very hard push against the cloth.

A huge rat? Appa instinctively realised this was no rat. Its force was much more than that of a mere rat. Appa loosened the cloth and left it a bit slack. The next time the creature pushed, part of its neck appeared briefly under the edge of the cloth. Appa used both hands to grab the neck of the creature through the cloth, and then lifted it out in his right hand. Only then did he realise that what he had caught was a cobra. Appa's friend took to his heels in terror. The snake was a long one, about Appa's height, and it was hissing ferociously. Appa could feel its fury through the cloth in which he held its neck. Appa had caught a snake all right. But now came the dilemma of what to do with it. How could he let it go unharmed while ensuring that it would also let him go unharmed? There seemed to be no way out except to kill the snake.

In Appa's mind, the urgent need for money battled against his natural fear. If he did not pay his fee and take the exam this time, he would be age-barred and would never have a future. If he were to kill the snake and sell its skin, he could perhaps earn enough to meet the exam fee. His fear of the snake took a back seat as his thoughts turned to strategy. If he beat the snake to death, the skin would be damaged and worth nothing. So Appa started squeezing the body of the snake with his left hand. The next moment the snake had coiled its massive body around Appa's left arm and was crushing it so hard that the bones of his arm were in danger of cracking. Appa used his right hand to try and pull the snake away. It was impossible. Neither could he fling it away and run to safety, because it was too tightly wrapped.

Appa decided that even if the battle meant splintered bones for him, he would kill the snake by crushing its head. It was a battle to the death...whose death was the question. That was the day Appa became closely acquainted with all aspects of snakes... the slippery body, the coldness, fear, excitement, disgust, cruelty, wrath.

Unable to bear the pain in his arm, Appa started biting the snake. Blood oozed from it. It tasted like sap from a banana plant at the tip of his tongue. Suddenly the thought flashed into his mind..maybe the snake's blood is poisonous. He stopped biting it.

Although Appa's bites had not harmed the snake, its ferocity began to wane. It was slowly dying. Even after it was dead it took Appa more than half an hour to uncoil its body from his arm. After his victory over the snake that day, Appa lost all fear of snakes. He sold the snake skin, paid the exam fee, passed his course and embarked on his career. In his mind, the slaying of the snake was synonymous with success in life.

At nights, kraits could be seen cautiously peeping out through openings in the rubble piles around the house. Appa considered these snakes unworthy of his attention. As for the *vazhalai* snakes that hid under the Holy Mother's statue in the backyard, and the vipers, Appa was always ready to finish them off. He would display the dead snake and announce with a laugh, 'It sought moksha. It has gone to its Maker.' Amma would frown in displeasure. 'This sort of thing is not good,' she would say.

Aatha had left date palm fruits for ripening in my book

bag in the cupboard. They ripened into a bright chilli red. To my mind, they resembled snake eggs. The snake had coiled its body protectively around the fruits and was guarding them. Aatha plunged her hand into the bag and took out a handful of the fruits. I begged her not to eat them, but Aatha declared that they were very sweet and fleshy and delightfully cool.

The night had adorned itself with the waning moon and was flaunting its beauty. Amma was away from town. Appa was in his room and Aatha was asleep in the koodam. I was also in the koodam, stretched out on a bench and watching TV. Aatha, with her sheet drawn up to her chest was sleeping with her face turned towards the TV set, and my bench was right next to her. Suddenly, from under the bench came a *sarrsarr* sound like sand being rubbed against the floor. I bent to take a look—and got the shock of my life. On the floor just beyond the bench and very close to where Aatha lay, a coiled snake was spinning slowly around. I sat up very gently and silently. I was soaked in sweat. I couldn't find my voice to let out any kind of warning. I was paralysed with fear. I understood the impending danger in the situation. I told myself to stay calm. If I were to raise an alarm, Appa would hear me and come rushing out of his room to investigate. But before that Aatha would wake up. What if the snake reacted before Aatha did? What if it bit her? So I could not make a noise. Limp with fear and tears, I huddled on the bench.

The snake lifted its head and surveyed its surroundings. I was on tenterhooks lest Aatha started stirring in her sleep. The snake continued to raise and lower its head alternately and go around in coiled circles. As it did so it moved slowly along the floor till its coiled body was partly on Aatha's mat. And still I sat inert, bathed in sweat and tears, frozen with dread. At this stage it would be even more dangerous to make any kind of noise. But my mind was in turmoil. It sent up the same endless prayer with folded hands for divine intervention in this perilous moment: please don't let Appa wake up, please don't let Aatha move.

Aatha had a habit of moving and turning quite a lot in her sleep. But tonight she seemed to be in deep slumber after a tiring day, and she did not move at all. What a mercy! The sound from the TV was another factor in the scene, but there was no way I could reduce the volume. In my mind I pleaded desperately with the snake: 'Go away, please go away from my Aatha.'

In the light from the TV set, the coiled snake appeared to my eyes like a dark shadow. The snake, which had raised its head earlier, now lowered it and started crawling across Aatha. Where was I? What had happened to me? Why could I not move? The snake climbed over Aatha's thigh and set a diagonal course towards the TV. For whatever reason, perhaps because she had pulled a sheet over herself, Aatha slept on undisturbed.

I rose and stood near the bench. Many plans were tumbling through my mind. The moment the snake had crossed over Aatha and moved away I would wake her, or drag her to safety, or maybe drag the whole mat along with her on it.

I don't know if I felt fear at that moment. What was

uppermost in my mind was to somehow save my Aatha who was everything to me.

By now, half the snake's body had crossed over to the other side of Aatha. I waited in tense anticipation, like a predator waiting to leap on its prey. Quite unexpectedly, the snake abruptly changed direction and started crawling right along the length of Aatha's sleeping form. I froze. My legs went numb. I don't know how it happened, but I turned into a living statue. I was sure my Aatha was going to die, and it would be my fault. I crumbled and melted and was swirled away into nothingness. The snake could strike Aatha at any moment. It could choose a spot anywhere on her body, wherever its head happened to be. As though bound hand and foot and immersed in deep water, I stood tongue-tied and helpless.The snake traversed Aatha's chest, wriggled on to her shoulder and moved towards her neck. I was steeling myself for any eventuality. As the snake crept on to her bare neck, Aatha was disturbed from the depths of her sleep. She suddenly turned over. I rushed forward and swooped down to try to catch the snake. Between Aatha's movements and mine, we found we had somehow managed to push the creature away to a spot under the TV.

By this time I had found my voice. I yelled and shouted as I tugged and pulled on Aatha to get her to safety. I brought her to a safe distance, got her to her feet, and turned on the light. Appa was standing there in shocked silence. Aatha had no clue what had occurred, except that there had been some kind of commotion.

Appa continued his statue-like stance. Aatha was

trembling all over, and I held her hand tight in mine. The cold feel of the snake was still tingling my nerve ends, and the palms of my hands that had touched it felt frozen and wet like a lump of ice.

Appa emerged from his state of shock and asked in an agitated voice, 'Enna ma, what happened?' I pointed wordlessly towards the floor under the TV set. The snake crawled along the edge of the wall unhurriedly and disappeared through the drainpipe. Appa stood and watched it, making no move to try to kill it. I was surprised to see Appa's uncharacteristic reaction. Why had he let the snake escape?

Aatha, who had been unaware of most of the drama, now began to realise that the unseen object that had touched her neck must have been a snake. She was going through the emotions of a child that had just escaped the clutches of the dreaded *sadukka bhootham*. Somehow borrowing some words from the darkness of the night, and stuttering in fear and dread, I related the snake saga to Appa and Aatha.

Amma returned the next day. When she heard what had happened, she declared that this was a very bad development. So far the snakes had not bothered the people in the house, but now this one had actually crawled over her mother-in-law. She was strongly of the opinion that it was an omen of something disastrous awaiting us.

But some of the people of the town had a different opinion. They said that having a snake crawl upwards along one's body from the feet towards the head signalled prosperity and wealth for the family. As it happened, the rooster that

Amma had been raising as her ritual annual sacrifice to snakes had disappeared from our backyard. Amma had clung to the hope that it would reappear somehow, but it did not. In the light of new developments, she felt very apprehensive. She promised a variety of offerings to Vanathu Chinnappar and vowed to observe a fast. Appa was constantly ranting about how he would certainly crush the snake to death the next time he laid eyes on it, and this added fuel to Amma's indignation. She turned on him and spoke passionately. 'That snake crawled over your mother without harming her. It turned you both into helpless statues and calmly went on it way. Can you not understand its power?' Appa merely chuckled and moved away.

During the next one week no one saw any snake inside or outside the house. In fact Amma was upset that she had not spotted any snake on Tuesday and Friday as she had always done.

Amma made arrangements to replace the sacrificial rooster that had gone missing. Appa continued to repeat his intention to kill the snake at the first available opportunity. Amma visited the pujari* of the Mariamman temple to ask whether it was a good omen or a bad one if a snake crawled over one's body. The pujari expressed his opinion that this event signalled a threat to someone's life. He strongly advised her to offer prayers to the Puttru Mariyamman, the divine guardian of snakes' nests.Amma pledged offers of cooked rice to Chinnappar and kanji to Mariamman.

The total absence of snakes for a whole week was baffling. Even the rat snakes that always roamed around the backyard and the grass snakes that crawled in and out through the boundary fence were missing. It was as if some of the usual inmates of the house had gone away for a visit. The backyard had the aura of an abandoned place. This sudden withdrawal of the snakes from our lives, their impassive silence, their spurning of us, added to Amma's feeling of dread.

Then, in the dead of night, there was a commotion from the hen coop outside Appa's window. The pet ducks that we kept in the coop were quacking non-stop. We had raised this pair of ducks for many years, the male snow-white all over, the female with a mix of white and rust. Even though their ducklings died, these two had survived. The moment anyone stepped out of the house in the morning the ducks would run quacking after him. Aatha would hold conversations with the ducks as she fed them their meal of oats and grains. At dusk they would go back on their own into their coop for the night. They were like the babies of the household, and were showered with indulgence and affection by everyone.

When they started quacking that night, our first thought was that a mongoose or wild cat had got into the coop. Appa picked up a flashlight and a stick and went outside to investigate. It was pitch dark outside, so Appa turned on the light outside the front door.

In a short while Appa re-entered the house and woke us all. We went outside. One of the ducks lay dead. The other was struggling in the last throes of life. Both bodies had turned blue. As the duck took its last breath Amma said,

'As the pujari predicted, lives have been sacrificed. But by the grace of Chinnappar no humans have been harmed. Oh Vanathu Chinnappar...'

Even as Amma was uttering this, Appa brought the dead snake that he had just slaughtered, threw it in front of the dead ducks, and went back into the house.

I ran to my room and opened my cupboard in the darkness. The snake was shuddering in pain. Marks of the blows it had received were visible all over. At the end of the street, in the thick of night, a snake charmer started playing on his pipe. The sound fell upon my ears as waves, and reached the snake as vibrations. It cringed and trembled in terror. I bent and whispered something to it. In gratitude and delight, the snake came out and jumped into my arms. It climbed on to me and wrapped itself around me. We embraced in joy.

Glossary

Koodam: Central hall in traditional South Indian homes

Aatha: Grandmother (father's mother)

Siriyanangai and Periyanangai: Varieties of indigenous herbal plants with bitter leaves

Vanathu Chinnappar: Literally 'Saint of the sacred forest' who is believed to have lived in the 1st century C.E. Also known as St.Paul of Thebes in the Eastern Catholic tradition
Vazhalai snake: A species of ground snake
Moksha: release from the cycle of birth and death, in Hindu and Jain religious beliefs
Sadukkabhootam: A spirit that guards a crossroad. It is referenced in the classic Tamil epic Silappadhikaaram, the celebrated Jain Tamil epic of Kannagi and Kovalan
Pujari: Temple priest

ANNAACHI

BAMA

"Seems to be a madcap, this fellow. His *ayyan* and *amma* are so docile---what a fate to have this good-for-nothing donkey as their son!"

Maadathi sounded angry and fed up. Muthurathinam cut in: "See, that's the thing---all the children in that family are like this. At least something can be done with the others, but this fellow...this Ammaasi.... you can't tackle him this way, you can't tackle him that way..totally hopeless case.

Thaayamma was sitting stringing beads nearby. "Who?... Oh, you're talking about Irulaayi's grandson. He is an odd fellow all right."

Ammaasi was about twenty. As all the girls passing by on the street acknowledged, he was a fine figure of a lad. The adults of the village disliked him wholeheartedly. But the young boys adored and idolised him.

Well-grown for his age and with an impressive black

Translated by Malini Seshadri
Original Source: Annaachi. From *Dalit Sirukathai Thoguppu* edited by P Sivakami (Sahitya Akademi, 2014)

moustache, Ammaasi was a good-looking fellow. A good physique. When he laughed his teeth glistened and gleamed like the little leaping fish in flooded paddy fields. Who knows what the fellow used for cleaning his teeth? Even when he seemed to be talking drivel, there was always truth in what he said. He gave the outward impression of an idle loafer, indifferent and unconcerned. But he was actually very aware of things.

Day in and day out, only disparaging comments were made about him. I used to tell myself, people have not really understood him, that's why they talk such negative stuff about him. To this day I believe that what he did was honest, was right. After all, I got the whole story directly from him.

One morning at dawn, when I had gone near the irrigation tank to relieve myself, I spotted him. That is when we got to talking. I just asked, what's happening, what's up? He responded with a smile and went on to relate the details of events in the same cheerful manner.

"*Ey, macchaan*, tell me...what's wrong with what I did. Yesterday I worked in Parusuramar Ayya's field and got home early. I had some koozhu to eat and then went out again and got on the bus to go to Vettiyakallu."

"But why did you want to go to Vettiyakallu" I asked.

"Listen, *macchaan*, I'll tell you...that sissy shopkeeper fellow said some well-digging work is available in Vettiyakallu, so I went to check it out. It was a huge problem even to get onto the bus at the stand. Such a crowd..."

"Did you get into a fight with anyone in trying to

squeeze into the bus?"

"You are a pain, *macchaan*! Why don't you listen to the whole story without butting in?"

Being well aware of his nature, I stayed patient. "All right, I won't interrupt. Tell me."

I looked intently at him in anticipation of what might follow.

"In spite of that milling crowd I somehow managed to get into the bus and find a seat. That Chandrasekar also got into the bus. You're wondering whom I'm talking about? You know the fields in which we work for wages? He is the upper-caste landlord for those fields...yes that same Chandrasekar. Do you know what he said as soon as he saw me? Listen, I'll tell you the dialogue that took place between us...word for word."

'Ey, de, aren't you that Maadasamy's son?'

'Yes, I am Maadasamy's son.'

'Ey, don't you know who I am?'

'Why wouldn't I know you? Of course I do. You're Chandrasekar, right?'

Ammaasi paused to pick up the edge of his dhoti and reach into the pocket of his shorts. He extracted a beedi and lit it.

"You're wondering why I'm lighting a beedi now? During that conversation on the bus we were smoking and puffing smoke all the time while we talked. I am repeating it now to capture that memory," declared Ammaasi.

I showed my annoyance. "Enough of all the drama and acting, da. Get on with it."

"Okay *macchaan*, listen.... So then he said..."

'You recognize me and still you are sitting? Get up and let me sit down.'

'I had to scramble in and squeeze through the crowd to get this seat. My stop is close by at Nettiyakallu. After I get off you can sit here.'

'Ey...so you're going to Nettiyakallu...get up, da. Move! When your Ayya is standing, how dare you show disrespect by sitting?'

'Ayya? You? My Ayya is right now ploughing your fields. When did you become my Ayya? Even if you stand upside down in protest, there is no way I am giving up the seat.'

By this point in Ammaasi's narration, his beedi had burnt down to a stub. He threw it away and burst into merry laughter. The expression on his face, a mix of mischief and humour, brought a smile to my lips.

I urged him to continue. "So you didn't get up at all right through the ride?"

"Jackpot! Of course I didn't get up. But do you think it ended there? Listen.."

Then, altering his voice suitably, Ammaasi picked up his story where he had left off.

'Eley...you are misbehaving with the hand that feeds you. You don't show even a speck of the gratitude and respect your father does. In the presence of the landlord the farm labourers, the pariahs stand respectfully at a distance. What does an upstart like you know about all that.'

'Yo, when I say I will not get up I mean it. If you carry on further with this, you will end up losing face.'

"I didn't say anything more. He kept muttering under his breath. I got off at Nettiyakallu. Now the elders on our street are scolding me for what happened."

"But how did the news get to the village so fast?" I asked.

"Oh, don't ask about that...such a wretched thing. It turns out that the same evening Chandrasekar told my father about it and told him to discipline me. My Ayya made such a ruckus about it at home that now the whole street is talking about nothing else."

I remarked, "The women folk in our village can't stop chattering....witches. *After all, when the landlord is standing, how can a pariah boy dare to sit? How presumptuous!.Arrogant fellow. His day of reckoning is fast approaching.....*"

Ammaasi laughed.

"Oh, worse than that, *macchaan*. Do you know what that old Paniyaramuthu said? '*Landlords are like gods for us. Without them, can we even survive? These young fellows are so foolish...deadbeats. There's a saying.... the dog you feed will never harm you. But this dog is pouncing and trying to bite the hand that feeds it. If the landlords set their minds to it, they will knock out all your teeth...*'

"I couldn't help laughing when I heard the old man ranting. When I laughed he scolded me some more. I came away laughing," said Ammaasi, laughing all over again while relating it.

Within a week of this commotion dying down, another round of street gossip started up about Ammaasi's misdeeds. But he went about here and there totally heedless, as though nothing had happened. So then I called him and asked,

"*Empa*, what have you done now?"

His response was evasive. "*Macchaan*, this evening the whole village is going to meet. Be there. They are going to interrogate a dangerous murderer and then hang him to death."

"That's okay, let them have a village meet. But what about you? What did you do?"

"I am the one they are going to interrogate, *macchaan*. So be sure to come," said Ammaasi.

I persisted with my question, "What's the accusation against you this time? Tell me...I'd like to know."

"You see, *macchaan*...a couple of days ago Muthu Karuppan uncle asked me to go and water landlord Jayasankar's fields."

"That's right...," I said, "I saw you setting off dressed up very smartly and with spade in hand. The way you looked, I was wondering if you were on your way to get a new handle for your spade."

"No teasing, *macchaan*, please. *Ey*, what's wrong with dressing up neatly when going to work? In fact, I gave Muthirulu a rupee to iron my shirt for me that morning."

"Yes, I noticed it was not crumpled.....but tell me the story."

"When I reached the field, Jayasankar was standing near the pump. When he saw me with the spade, he started talking to me." Having reached this juncture in his story, Ammaasi altered his voice for dramatic effect to describe the conversation.

'*Elai, I told Muthukaruppan who lives on your street to send me someone to water my fields. It's getting late. No fellow has turned up till now.'*

'Muthukaruppan uncle asked me to go and do the job. That's why I've come.'

'You don't look like a fellow who has come to work in the field. You've turned up dressed as if is an office job. You're that troublemaker fellow. Did he send you because he couldn't find anyone else?'

'Enga, now what do you want? You want your fields watered, right? How does it matter to you how I am dressed?'

'Elai, do you know what the time is? Turning up just now......as if he's travelled all the way from some distant place.'

'Annaachi, you're the one with a wrist watch. I don't have one. So you're the one who has to tell me what the time is. I must get a watch as soon as possible. After I get one and wear it, I can tell you the time, Annaachi.'

I was so amused by Ammaasi's narration and his facial expressions that I burst out laughing.

Ammaasi said, "Hold on...listen to the whole thing... When I addressed him as Annaachi, you should have seen his face. He became furious. He snarled at me:

'Ennelai, What did you say? You called me Annaachi? Who is Annaachi? Whose Annaachi am I? How dare a low pariah call me Annaachi!'

So I said *'Please control your words. Otherwise I will respond likewise and you will feel humiliated. If you didn't want me to work you could have just told me to go away. Why all this .... talk...?'*

"That was it. I left the place immediately and came home. Who knows what lies he told people...now they have called a meeting about it."

"You're certain to be punished today," I remarked. "After all you used curse words to the landlord."

"Oh...*macchaan*...you thought that is what the meeting is about? No, no. It's because I addressed that man as 'Annaachi'. That is the big crime they are going to discuss."

That evening the meeting was convened. The Headman of the village spoke. He said, "*Elai*, Ammaasi, what is our caste and what is the landlord's caste? Who is allowed to address whom as 'Annaachi'? What an ignorant fool you are, da."

Ammaasi said, "We are Parayars; he is a Naicker. And yes, I did address him as 'Annaachi'. But why have you called a meeting just to talk about that?" He scratched his head in a gesture of apparent puzzlement.

All the young men in the crowd laughed in glee at Ammaasi's reply. The Head tried to control his annoyance. "Look, I don't want to get into a long discussion with you. Just give me a straight answer. Why did you call the landlord 'Annaachi'?

Ammaasi's reply was swift. "He is older than me in age. That's why I said 'Annaachi'. If he had been younger I'd have called him 'Thambi'.

The younger crowd laughed even more boisterously this time.

"This fellow is not easy to tackle. Look at the way he talks...defiant fellow," remarked the Deputy Headman.

The Headman started talking in a grave tone: "*Elai*, we haven't called you here to entertain us. In all these years has any one of us parayan labourers used a kinship name to address a landlord? But you young fellow..... born just yesterday....... you are creating such a commotion. Admit it, wasn't it wrong on your part to address him as 'Annaachi'?"

Suddenly Ammaasi also took on a serious air. "There was nothing wrong in what I said. It's not as if I was claiming to be an uncle or brother-in-law seeking a marriage alliance with his son or daughter. I just addressed him in a normal way as 'Annaachi'. Why are you making such a big deal of it? Last week when I addressed the scavenger Irulappan as 'Annaachi' you all criticised me for addressing him that way because he is a lowly Kora fellow. But now you are contradicting yourselves by blaming me because I addressed a Naicker man the same way. As old Poovathi always says, 'In the dung from a donkey, what's the difference between the front part and the back part?' All dung is the same dung. All humans are the same."

Having spoken his piece, Ammaasi abruptly left and went home.

People were left staring at him dumbfounded.

THE UNIQUE LETTER

RAVIKUMAR

Editor's Note: *The title of the original story is ழ, a character in the Tamil script read with a voiced retroflex approximant sound. Denoted as 'zha' in translation, it is close to the sound of the letter 'r' in the word 'red' in native English speech. Tamil is the only language that has an exclusive character in its written script for this sound. In fact, the word 'Tamil' should be pronounced as 'thamizh', with the voiced retroflex approximant at the end.*

"What's happening there, *pa*?" Adheethan asked with eager eyes. I looked in the direction he was pointing.

A man lay spreadeagled. Two people stood on either side of him, pulling the ends of a rope tied around his neck. His face was contorted in pain, eyes bulging and mouth hanging open. Another man held his legs apart and inserted a needle into the man's erect phallus. A few policemen stood around, with serious eyes like those of doctors around an operation table. The image resembled a painting in its lighting and

---

Translated by V Ramakrishnan
Original Source: Short story, Zha published in Arangetram magazine, 1994

clarity. The photographer who took the picture must have been an expert.

"That man is ill and the doctors are treating him," I replied, turning Adheethan's face away from the sickening picture. But his head involuntarily returned to it. My shirt was soaked with sweat despite the air-conditioning, the low drone of which seemed to instruct us to stay quiet. I felt the silence in the room spreading and settling heavily on me like molten wax. I thought I heard the moans and screams from the pictures on the wall, and shuddered.

Adheethan was seated on my lap. Ruffling his hair with my fingers, I tried to focus on the strange calm that his presence induced in me. Yet, the next moment, an anxiety about what was going to happen crept up my spine.

I observed it only when I entered this room: the investigation office was run completely by women. Their olive green uniforms made even those pretty women look menacing. With faces as hostile and severe as their starched uniforms, they walked around like machines in straight lines.

I couldn't stop my eyes from grazing over the walls. Huge, colorful pictures had been set in a line on the plain walls—illustrations of methods of torture used in investigations.

It brought back memories of my childhood. There used to be a calendar in my teacher's house with illustrations of the various punishments administered in Hell. There was one of women impaled on long poles being dragged towards a vat of boiling oil for the sin of adultery. That was the first time I had seen grown women naked. Those images never frightened me. In fact, they held a strange allure. But perhaps due to my anxiety, the pictures in this room kindled a fear of punishment.

I never imagined I would end up in an interrogation room. The more I thought about it, the angrier I felt with my wife.

I had explicitly asked her not to let anyone into the house. These people had come in saying they needed to note our electricity metre readings. That had landed us here now!

Chaos had broken out after the Elder Guru of the country died suddenly last week. Following an inquiry, authorities claimed that the death was caused by a peel of a *vaazhai pazham* that lay on the Guru's path, and suspected that the people of the town of Paazh were behind this conspiracy. Since the unique 'zha' sound was the common thread between the words Paazh and *vaazhai pazham*, they also came to the conclusion that the 'Language War' movement had a part in the plot.

The Government made the announcement two days ago: the letter 'zha' had been removed from the language and any further use of it by anyone would be deemed an act of sedition; as a replacement, the letter 'sha' had been recommended.

Never did I imagine that it would be followed by such measures.

How could anyone have thought that forensics experts would raid every house to check if someone was still using the banned letter?

I looked at the picture hanging in the middle of the wall. It was one of Krishna preaching to Arjuna, with the following words written below: “You pay tribute to God through sacrifices. God loves you for it. It is by becoming one with him that you attain an elevated state.” Was it meant to prepare me for whatever awaited me?

The door connecting this room to the next opened noiselessly and a policeman emerged from the other side.

“Are you Kumar?”

“Yes, that’s me,” I stood up. He gestured for me to follow him, and walked past the door through which he had emerged. I took Adheethan’s arm and entered the other room. It felt like a different space. I couldn’t decide if it was a hall or a courtroom. Its style was an amalgam of modern architecture and the style of palaces I had seen only in old movies.

On a pedestal in the middle of the room, there sat a man dressed in a saffron-coloured uniform. One could tell from his bearing that he was a high-ranking official. Adheethan and I were guided into a cage-like witness box.

I heard something like a temple bell ring in the distance. The interrogation began as if on cue.

“Don’t you know of the Government’s order?” the official asked in a kind voice.

“I know, sir. It was announced on the TV,” I replied. My body’s trembling betrayed the fear I was trying so hard to conceal.

“Then how did this happen?” he asked, and pressed a button. On the opposite wall, an image appeared. The letter ‘zha’ was scribbled all over in a familiar handwriting. The letter ‘i-’ also appeared occasionally. It all suddenly made sense now. This was Adheethan's work! That was a wall in our home! With the crayons that Arulappan had given as a birthday gift, Adheethan had scribbled all over the wall.

"How beautifully he writes the letter 'i-'... Look how perfect his 'zha' is! His strokes have an artistic touch to them," Arulappan had said when he bought the crayons.

"My son wrote this on our wall to practise the letters he learnt at school. And... also... he did it last month," I stammered, pointing at Adheethan.

"You train your child to draw graffiti on walls?" The kindness in his voice had disappeared, and it was now replaced by suspicion.

"No, nothing like that... He's just a little boy. He did it by himself... He didn't mean anything by it, sir."

"We checked at his school as well. His class teacher confirmed that he's the only student who can write that letter so well. How do you explain that?"

"There's no particular reason, sir. He's just practised it so much that he does it well." My voice broke pitifully.

"We have looked into your records. There are no remarks so far. Since this is your first offense, we are letting you go with a warning. You'll have to make Sanskrit his second language. And whitewash your walls immediately and get a certificate from the Forensics after they inspect your house. Don't let us catch you for such an offense again. You must know what the sentence is for sedition now, don't you? So, you'd better be careful!"

Not knowing how to respond, I nodded.

The kind smile reappeared on his face now. "You can

leave now, son!" He raised his arm as if blessing us.

The policeman who led me signalled with a nod, and I followed him with Adheethan. I was happy that they had let us go. I had not expected the interrogation to end so quickly. I wondered if Adheethan's presence with me was the reason. I was, for some reason, convinced that they wouldn't punish children.

We came out of the interrogation office. The city was as busy as it always was. I wanted to buy something for Adheethan.

"Do you want to eat something?"

"No."

"Do you want to buy some toys—" I began to ask, but stopped abruptly. I didn't know where it would land us if he asked for a toy gun.

"No, *pa*," he said. Thank God!

"Shall we go home, then?"

"Sure, *pa*."

We walked to catch a tram.

"*Pa*... Can I not study 'a-' for 'amma', 'aa-' for 'aasiriyar' anymore?" he asked.

"Let's go home and talk. You must not ask about anything now. You're a good boy, aren't you? Listen to your *appa* now," I replied, warily looking around. Luckily, we caught a tram soon after.

Glossary

vaazhai pazham - ripe banana

BRO 'T'

PRATIBHA JEYACHANDRAN

Then Jesus looked at them and said: 'Take ye away the stone'.

Lazarus' sisters replied: 'Lord, the stench will be great for he hath been dead four days.'

When the stone had been rolled away, Jesus called: 'Lazarus! Come forth!'

Whereupon, shedding his grave cloth, Lazarus stepped out of the tomb alive.

This part of John's Gospel was running through my mind as I made my way along the Upper Bazaar Road, Ooty*. That was when something totally unexpected happened.

'Brother! Brother 'T''. The familiar voice from my distant past shook my composure.

A name that had once been part of me, inseparable from my existence like my very breath, steeped into the depth of

---

Translated by Malini Seshadri
Original Source: Saho D, *Dalit Sirukathai Thoguppu*: An Anthology of Dalit Short Stories compiled by P Sivakami (Sahitya Akademi, 2014)

my consciousness...and later lost, the name that society had plucked away from me.... it was now reminding me of my lineage, my forgotten past. My name. 'T'.

Not only in my class, not only in my school or college, but even in my town I was the owner of the exclusive name 'T'. During those early years of fulfilment, of dreams and joy, those years that slipped through time like a slippery palm fruit slips down one's throat, the name had stayed with me and attached itself to me.

Every year, the student who took first place in the final exam at the end of school would have his name permanently inscribed on the Roll of Honour. The board at my school read:

YEAR	NAME	MARKS OBTAINED
1967	M.Sivapaadha Sundaram	402
1968	C.Selvaraj	417
1969	A.Vijayaraghavan	396
1970	A.Mariappan	431
1971	K.Rajkumar	379
1972	V.Sundarraj	391
1973	V.T.	419

On the school wall, redolent with the scent of neem, is deeply etched a name: 'T'.

A few portions from my scribbles (uncensored).

I

It was a holiday. As we were chatting idly in the *chavadi** Elango brought up an idea. Then we decided that it would be better if around ten of us went as a group. We had no money. The thought of Adaikalayya came to mind. He would not hesitate to part with his money for this sort of thing. Sure enough we got the money. When we entered the tea shop, as a group, the local customers dispersed hastily. We placed orders for ten teas. The shop had only three *vatta** cups available for serving people like us. Tea arrived in the three cups. None of us drank the tea.. Vellaiamma went outside for about five minutes and returned. Noticing that the cups had not yet been emptied she must have realised there was no other alternative. So she brought tea in glass tumblers for the rest of us. We paid the bill and left, feeling victorious for having achieved what we had set out to do. This was the topic of discussion in the village for a whole week. It was rumoured that Vellaiamma received a belt-whipping at the hands of Kondal Reddiar that day. But from then onwards, the tea shop stopped using those kinds of cups.

II

My family decided that we should attend the convention. I was rather unhappy, but at the same time pleasurably excited. The pleasure arose from the thought that, after the evangelical session in the evening, I could go with my gang (those friends who had not yet attained salvation) to a night show of a movie. In fact, even the afternoon three o'clock show was not ruled out. Later on, when the congregation was moved by the spirit and deep in prayer, we could slip away unnoticed and smoke weed. I would not have my mother often demanding to smell my breath in suspicion, with the underlying threat of severe punishment. Also, there would be many girls there to look at (to make sheep's eyes at). In the Bible, Abraham introduced his wife Sarah to strangers as his sister. 'My wife who is my sister' are the words of the text. So we had a shorthand term to refer to our 'sight sisters', the ones we were ogling. They were our 's. s'.

We would get back to the convention tent from a late movie show and flop into bed. Then, within what seemed hardly any time at all, two Brothers would come by beating drums to wake us. Five a.m. The drum beats were accompanied by a song offering too:

'Let us awake
Let us be full of life
Till the end of the world.....'

It was all such a drag. Wearily we would brush our teeth, form groups and set out on the streets to spread the Gospel. We would move around half asleep. Some groups would have more s.s. in them. It was preferable to get into one such group.

Martin was in a group with a lot of s.s. Lucky fellow! He played the guitar too...so what's left to say...? He was always surrounded by s.s. At such times I would yearn to learn how to play the guitar. But then, what would be the use of that? It's not as if they will ask me to perform for an audience...a person like me who had not attained salvation. Even if I were to get salvation, I had to obtain the blessings of Warrier, the head of the Youth Wing before I could dream of any kind of recognition. Only the Nadar boys such as Jagan and Lazarus got all the love and respect of Warrier.

And the mischief they got into with the s.s.....the less said about that the better.

When it came to VBS (Vacation Bible School) and Conventions, those youth were the heroes. We were cast as the villains...fit only to move the tables and help in putting up the tents. That Youth Wing leader fellow Warrier deserves a sound thrashing some day. He is very polite when he talks to his preferred people and his relatives, *Vanga, Ponga*; to us it is *Va pa, Po pa* or, to the younger ones, *Va da, Po da**.

One Friday evening, after the Youth Wing meeting, Warrier was chatting with some of the chosen few among the young men.

"What's happening? Why is it that our young members are not paying attention to Bible Studies? Look at the New Street fellows...they're very smart. The new pastor is their man. He takes only those fellows along for everything. House visits, retreats, evening prayers...they are the only ones with him. He visits our people's houses only very rarely. If we do nothing about this, these fellows may get into the Church committees and start selecting their *naatamai**. Something must be done to make him change his ways.'

A young boy who lived on New Street happened to overhear Warrier's comments. He came and told me what he had heard. For any festival or celebration, they are the ones coming forward to offer donations. They are all well to do people. We're not like that. We sweat all day just to stay alive.

That's why every pastor is a supporter of theirs. But our pastor is not like that. So they're itching to get back at us.

Sure enough, the very next month after the Convention, our pastor was replaced.

III

As a kind of introduction to our village, here is how my grandfather describes it. (The words and names within brackets are mine)

When I was a boy, there were only a hundred families in the village. I'm talking about our south village alone. In the north village there were another hundred or so families. It lay between Aruppotai (Aruppukottai) and Virudhupatti (Virudhunagar), a wasteland area Palamenam, that is Palavanatham. No proper roads at that time, only mud paths. You might see one vehicle passing by in the morning, and maybe another in the evening. Vehicles wearing faces in front. The earliest buses were the Shanmugam buses and the Meenambikai ones. They were the ones run by the Naickers and Chettiyars of Aruppukottai. Those were the days when people used to gather just hoping to see a passing car. We boys used to be in Kattukal Moopar's garden, perched on the top branches of a neem tree that offered the perfect vantage point. Very early in the morning, when the dawn sky was just beginning to redden, we would settle ourselves on the tree. We could spot an approaching bus from far away, even when it was still beyond the cactus bridge, close to Neeravy, where Mookaayi hanged herself to death. The bus would create a cloud of dust as it moved along. As it came closer, the swirling dust would obscure the road itself. We would clamber down from the tree, run into the village streets and announce that the bus would soon be here. Then we would hurry back to the road. The bus would move slowly through the village. We would run behind it, escorting it up to the Odhuvaar Bridge before returning.

Not many people from our south village travelled out for any reason. Once in a way the sons of the Chettiyar folk would go and see a matinee show at Virudhunagar. From the north village, as many as four or five would take the bus. They were government workers. The whole village knew who exactly had visited Virudhunagar and on which days they had done so. They also knew who had entertained a visitor. No visitor to our street arrived by bus. Those who lived fairly close by would carry food for the journey in a bundle on their heads and walk all the way. Those who lived in a neighbouring village would make a start in the morning, brushing their teeth with a twig as they went, and get here after making a stop to relieve themselves on the way. I would think to myself, some day I will get on that bus with all these other people. It never happened. We didn't have the means for it.

In the eastern part of the south village, there were about thirty families of Moopars. Only recently have they got this respectable label. Earlier the Reddiars and Naickers used to call them Valayans. They owned very little land. They worked as farm labourers, and in their spare time hunted squirrels. They would catch snakes, skin them, and sell the skins at Madurai. They cooked and ate the squirrels and white mice that they trapped. Late in the evening they would set out rabbit hunting. In the process they would sneak into farmlands and steal whatever they could. How else would they survive? The women worked as farm labourers. There was a man called Arihara Moopar who performed *paavai koothu** in the evenings. We folks from the south village would go to see him perform. The fee was two paise per head. He used to do a good job of it, singing to a proper beat and putting up a good show.

Further to the west were about ten houses of Chettiar families. Five houses of Pillais, four of Naickers. The rest of the families there were all Nadars. They were the ones who had prospered really well through money-lending. Bal Nadar started off by selling candy and dates. Even in this business he made enough money to build a pucca* house. A couple of others from their community set up small shops on the roadside.

In those days, adults who needed to go somewhere would ride a bicycle. That is when Periasamy Nadar bought four bicycles and set up a cycle shop. To start with, he had a bicycle of his own. As he moved around on it he started learning about things that could go wrong with bicycles. He taught himself how to repair a bicycle. Then he set up a shop. His was the very first cycle repair shop there. Other Nadars also set up other kinds of shops...eateries, general stores, betel nut booths and so on. Gradually, they had captured all the commercial activity in the area. Sangu Pillai was the only person from another community to set up shop in the south village. He opened a mixture and *sev** shop which did good business. Seeing this, Mara Nadar's wife Seeniamma set up a shop selling the same eatables on the opposite side of the road. Both shops were managed by the women of the family. There was never an occasion when a snack bought at Sangu Pillai's shop had to be discarded because it was spoilt.

Apart from these, the only other castes in the south village were our three—Pallans, Parayans and Chakkiliyans—living on the southern side of the road. Ayyo, those Pallan fellows! They don't want to be called Pallans. It makes them boiling mad to hear that term. They want to be known as Kudumbas. Why they protest being called Pallans and why it riles them so much I cannot understand. Among our three castes, it was only the Pallans who received some degree of respect from the higher caste people. As for the rest of us—they wouldn't hesitate even to attack us with sickles. Among them was a Pallan fellow called Karuppiah. He once murdered the son of a Reddiar and was sent to jail. Because he was referred to as a Pallan, on his way to prison he seems to have urged his caste youth, 'If anyone dares to put his tongue to his teeth and utter the term Pallan when he looks at us, go and break the fellow's teeth at once, *da*'. After that, the people of other castes were very wary about how they addressed the Pallans. But, to this very day, with all that aggression, the Pallans live in destitution. Their children are illiterate and they continue to roam around aimlessly, subsisting on occasional farm work. One wise fellow among them converted to Christianity and sent his children to school. One of his children is now a teacher. Another two sons took up I.T. courses and landed jobs somewhere near Tiruchi. Of all the houses on this south side of the road, his is the only one to get letters now and then by post. Now he has built his own house and is quite well off. Sometimes, when the priest is unable to come, this man fills in for him and conducts the prayers at church.

Our Parayan families are just ten. None of us did well in life. Only your son converted to Christianity, studied and earned the title of Veda Manickam (Jewel of the Scripture) and is now a teacher. He married a Christian girl of the same caste but unrelated to him.

There were about thirty Chakkiliyar families. They were the ones who were the drummers in funeral processions. They would perform *koothu* to the rhythm of drum beats. In fact, in all the villages the Chakkiliyars were the *koothu* artistes. Your uncle was a very good nadaswaram player. He went away to another village and made his living by playing his instrument. But here the Chakkiliyars are the drum players. Among all the castes, they are the ones who are most shabbily treated. They are also in the 'untouchable' category, like us. They look after the cattle of rich farm owners and do odd jobs to earn a jug of *koozhu**. These are the most destitute of all. To this day you cannot find a single fellow in this community who can read or write even a couple of words. Among the Chakkiliyar families in other villages, there are a few who have managed to get an education for their children. But here, in our village, not a single one.

Nowadays the population has grown large. The panchayat board office has got a radio and a TV. Even schools with classes right up to ten have been opened. Two cinema tents have appeared. You can no longer tell who's who in the village...lots of unfamiliar faces, buses brimming with passengers. But our people are still struggling, with not even a handspan of land to call their own. The Christians have also grown in number. Every Sunday long lines of them can be seen on their way to church, carrying bibles. But even more than our people, the Reddiars and Nadars also attend church. And the leader in the church is always only a Nadar.

IV

I was resting in the *chavadi* when Ramasamy, the son of Narayanan Mama, came by. He distributed chocolates to those who were around and announced that he had found a job. I was delighted to hear it. He was a member of the congregation; in fact he had even been baptised. At the baptism he was renamed as Rockland. In the church circles he was always addressed only as 'Rockland Brother'. His certificate still declares him to be a Hindu, and he got the job on the Scheduled Caste quota. That Sunday he bore witness in Church. He said Lord Jesus had felt sympathy for him and had ordained that he should get a job. He said it was the Lord's reward for his remaining true to Him and for his long sessions of fasting and prayer. 'Lord Jesus has brought me this victory. All hail to His name. Hallelujah!' he declared. 'Hallelujah' rose the chorus from the congregation.

That same evening, my mother cornered me. 'You have not yet become God's child. You will be able to get a job only if you get salvation.' I pointed out the list of others who had not been able to get jobs despite attaining salvation.

Amma was furious. 'If you go on talking against God like this you will never get a job. You will just roam around being an idler for ever,' were her damning words.

That night I placed a tape cot outside the house and lay down. I wept for hours.

Disrespected in the church, disrespected at home. If I just went on like this, drinking *kanji* and roaming around here and there, it would soon start to seem like a comfortable lifestyle. I would become a good-for-nothing.

I went to Prem's house at night and knocked on his door. His elder sister opened the door. Regina was a beautiful girl with ample breasts. 'Isn't Prem here?' I asked.

'He's asleep. Shall I wake him?' she asked. 'No, that's all right,' I said, and turned to leave.

'Wait, *pa*, if there's anything else you need, just ask me.'

Despite myself, my gaze shifted to her bosom. She grabbed me and pulled me towards her. She pressed my face against her breasts. The reek of sweat was overpowering; yet it felt soft and comfortable. I was trembling all over. Regina looked at me longingly. I bowed my head. We stayed that way for a while. I needed that. Then I detached myself from her embrace and prepared to leave.

'If you have any cash can you give me eight annas?' I asked. She asked me to wait, went inside and brought back one rupee for me. 'Is that enough?' she asked. A sense of shame swept over me. 'Come often,' she told me. I nodded, hurriedly came down the steps and walked away. I left the street where the Nadars lived and came to the main road.

People were on their way home after the night show. Stray dogs were barking everywhere. I bought tea at a tea shop. At the kiosk opposite I also bought four Charminar cigarettes. Then I went directly to the north village, to the home of Ocha Thevar. I pushed aside the front screen and called out 'Thevare!' 'Who is it at this hour?' 'It's me, T. I need you to give me something, a packet.' I handed him four annas. He verified carefully that it was indeed a genuine coin. He took out a palm-sized green pouch from his waist band and put the coin into it. Then he reached into a crevice in the tile roof of the verandah, produced a brown paper packet and handed it to me. It was very dark on the way back. There was not a soul about. I went and sat on the 'Seven Persons Bridge'. This was where seven people had once been brutally hacked to death. Everyone avoided sitting there alone at night. They would not even pass that way. Women and girls gave the place a wide berth. It was said that it was haunted by a ghost that asked for *sunnambu*, the slaked lime that is smeared on betel leaves.

There was a cool breeze. I took out the cigarettes, extracted the tobacco carefully, mixed it with some of the contents of the brown paper packet, and stuffed the mixture back gently into the cigarette paper rolls. After stuffing all the four cigarettes, there was still enough left in the packet for two more. I folded the packet away carefully in my bag. I took one of the doctored cigarettes and lit it.The smoke went down smoothly...much more smoothly than from an ordinary cigarette, which needs more of a dragging effort to get it down. This smoke slid in gently and made my body light as cotton wool, ready to take off and fly. I continued to draw in the smoke.

At a distance I saw two people approaching. This trip to the north village had made me audacious. I decided to make the ghost story about the bridge come true. I felt as if the universe was at my feet, ready to fulfil my every wish. Yet I stubbornly refused all the boons it was offering me. I want nothing, I declared. The two people were coming closer. Cigarette in mouth, I climbed onto the parapet of the bridge. I undid my white *dhoti*, took it off and waved it in the air above my head. 'Ghost! Ghost!' they screamed. They turned tail and fled without a backward glance. I got down, wrapped my *dhoti* around my waist, and went home.

The next morning, the streets were abuzz with the latest rumour. It was said that the previous night a ghostly spectre, breathing fire and spreading whitely all the way from ground to sky, was sighted on the Seven People Bridge. Two Naickers spotted it and ran away. They were so unnerved that they spent all night at a tea shop before venturing home.

V

Every fellow of my age had found a job and left the village. Except Brother S. He and I were the only ones left. We were ignored by everyone. My parents were approaching retirement age. I was not happy about hanging around idly at home. On some days I would get weeding work in the fields. Sometimes I would be hired to water Naicker's field. In a couple of months of this kind of work, the skin on my face turned very rough and dark.

I spent a few days as bookkeeper in the office of a match factory. One day, in the office, I was glancing at the newspaper when an item caught my eye. That news began to fester in my mind. My Sunday visits to church had reduced greatly. I had totally stopped attending bible classes, *tarrying meetings* and so on. Not that anyone bothered to ask me why I didn't attend. Earlier, even if I missed the meeting just one week, Warrier himself used to ask, 'Why didn't you come to the meeting, brother?' These days it felt as if I had been excluded from every social circle. My existence was of no value and no concern to anyone. The other Youth Club members were in good positions, with decent jobs. There were a lot of new youngsters too. It was an unsettling feeling, as if a whole generation had somehow disappeared within a short interval. I was introduced to the new batch of youngsters as one of them. But I felt embarrassed to mingle with them. I held back, and gradually dropped out of church activities totally. I would have still liked to be part of the group that went around the streets singing carols at Christmas time. Others in my family took part in the carols. My name never came up.

I used to meet Prem once in a while. He would bring a small packet of weed with him. We would sit near the community well and smoke the weed. Then back to the *chavadi* and bed.

The newspaper item that I had come across in the match factory office continued to gnaw at my mind. I tried to tell myself, 'What will I achieve by trying to change? What does it matter where I live? Whatever is fated to happen will happen anyway.' But anxiety had set in; I was growing older....

Brother S and I spoke about this, but couldn't come to any firm decision. It was in that situation that Johnson stepped in. He is now 'Vijaya Kumar'. He works in the Excise Department. He reported that corruption was rife there. An atmosphere had been created where it is acceptable, and saying no is not an option. Like us, he too had not got salvation.

'In Madras even the 'saved' ones are doing the same thing,' he told us. 'Otherwise, who will take you on for any job? Just pluck up courage and go and get it done, *Anna*.

My earlier resolve began to crumble. We had not learnt any trade. No income from farming either. Apart from the fact that I could read and write, what else was I fit for? At most I may be able to patch a puncture on a bicycle tyre. What kind of living could a man of my caste earn for himself in this village?

One Sunday, Brother S. and I set off for Madurai. A crowd had collected at the *Aadheenam* venue ahead of us. There were a few women among them. No one was talking to anyone else. As though realising that what they were doing was a matter to be ashamed of, they sat with bowed heads. There was an underlying anxiety about encountering someone familiar. Yet, having taken the plunge and come all the way, what was the use of worrying about things like that?

At last, once the prayer was over, everyone was given certificates and *prasaadam*. The next day, the news would be in the papers. People who had not bothered to acknowledge my existence up to then, turned up to meet me. The pastor also paid a visit. They scolded my father for letting me do this. My father said he didn't know anything about it, and went and lay down. Once the others had left, my father told me: 'You did the right thing. I joined the church when I was young only so that I could get an education. It suited me, and so I stayed with it. But the times have changed. You have changed your religion now so that you can get a job. Nothing wrong with that. The only sad part is, it means prostrating at the feet of the stone-idol worshippers as we were doing earlier. It's all right. People will say a thousand things. What do they care? They are ready to pay money to buy jobs, because they have the cash. Those who don't have ready cash have some land. What do we have except these bodies of ours? That's the only thing we can offer. You have gone and surrendered to them. So now it's time to forget the past life. Look ahead.'

My father said all this in an utterly calm voice. After he left, I was astonished at how he had taken the news. Within the Appa I thought I knew, there was another Appa like this one....an Appa whom I did not know at all!

VI

'Hello....you are...?'

'Can't you recognize me? I'm Brother Martin.'

'Martin? You've gone bald....What brings you here?'

'There was a prayer meeting at the Y.M.C.A. They invited me to come and speak. I welcomed the opportunity to look around this place. What do you do?'

'I'm a steno at Hindustan Photo Films. Why don't you drop in at my home?'

'Married?'

'Mm, yes. Love marriage. I married a Chettiar girl and we have a son.'

'Which church are you attending here?'

'I decided to leave all that behind me. I have a job that pays a decent salary. I am able to provide for my wife and child so that they are not in want. Beyond that, I don't know what I want to be. If it becomes necessary to choose what to become, I will choose. But for now my name is not 'T'. It is Kumar. Rajkumar.' I handed him my visiting card.

Lazarus has risen from the dead and emerged alive. This time without help from anyone.

Glossary

Ooty: Hill town in the Nigiri Hills, Tamil Nadu

Chavadi: A meeting place in villages where peasants assemble and chat and even sometimes take rest or sleep the whole night

Vatta cups: Disposable cups

Vanga, ponga: These are respectful forms of address. *Va pa, po pa* are less respectful; *va da, po da* are familiar forms of address

Naataamai: Village Headman

Paavai koothu: A form of shadow puppetry

Sev: A savoury snack

Koothu: Street theatre

Koozhu: Gruel

Dhoti: Traditional wrap-around lower garment for men

Tarrying meetings: Events in the Pentecostal church tradition at which those who have attained salvation congregate and pray together to experience the Holy Ghost

Anna: Literally 'elder brother' but used as a familiar form of address to an older man

Aadheenam: Hindu religious institution that used to hold sessions to accept converted Christians back into Hinduism if they so wished. They would be given certificates to this effect, which were helpful in getting Scheduled Caste certificates, and therefore jobs under quotas

Prasaadam: Ritual offering to deities in temples, distributed to devotees

YET ANOTHER RAINY SEASON

PABLO ARIVUKKUYIL

The rainy season had set in. The rains had strengthened gradually and poured all night long a couple of nights ago. As if that was not enough, there has been a relentless light shower for two whole days. Bleak as it was to feel the hot air and see the dried, cracked ponds in summer, one could at least step out of the house, walk a few miles to access the wells in Kollaikkaadu and fetch water for drinking and cleaning. But during the rains even daily activities come to a standstill. Firewood would have to be preserved from dampness. The old thatched roof would have to be replaced with millet hay, straw or at least dried palm sheaths. Otherwise, the rain would drip into the house and ruin the cow-dung-smeared floor. So difficult to take the cattle out for grazing. Since walking in the mire brings infections on their feet, some would fashion wooden slippers before they ventured out. Hats made out of woven coconut leaves

---

Translated by V Ramakrishnan
Original Source: Serukkuvaravukaaranin Soori *Dalit Sirukathai Thoguppu*: An Anthology of Dalit Short Stories compiled by P Sivakami (Sahitya Akademi, 2014)

may save people from light rains, but are of no use during a heavy downpour. Stepping out for nature's call would be so revolting that the whole body would shudder with disgust for having come out. Women go to the julifora forest, and men to the lake bund or cremation grounds for defecating. The stench of the feces-mixed-rain-water would be so strong as to pull out one's intestines. Watching the skies or the anonymous flowers that smile at us through dripping fences, we pinch our noses tight, finish our jobs and return. For those struggling to make ends meet, open grounds are toilets. How could someone destined to a dripping hut appreciate the rain? Rainy season is a time of daily struggle here.

She sat staring at the rain. Even in this rain, scrawny hens were roaming around on the street in search of food.

"When will *appa* come?" the child asked, looking at the photo on the wall. She struggled to answer. In order not to disappoint the child, she said, "He'll be home after a month, *pa.*" Patting him and singing a lullaby, she consoled the agitated child and put him to sleep.

Wasn't it the rainy season that had united her with her *mama* and made her a mother? It comes every year, digs out all the buried sweet memories and oozes with anguish, prodding the wounds from the past…

Tears flowed without her consent. It seemed as if everything had happened just yesterday. When Kathirvelu from the house opposite had come to her with the news, it was unbelievable. Grief had struck like lightning. How the village used to be! How beautiful the streets used to be! The death of one person had transformed the whole slum into an earthquake-hit land. How could they set the fire of grief on people who had served them for ages?! How could they mercilessly toss suckling infants into the fire? How? Thinking of those who, without conscience and compassion, had indulged in such inhuman violence, she dissolved into tears.

If the atrocities and murders committed by the landlords were listed, wouldn't it warrant an annihilation of not just them, but of all their descendents as well? But these poor people never even entertained such thoughts. The landlords could not tolerate that single attack that her husband and his companions had mounted on them. Was it fair to burn down the whole slum to retaliate for the action of one man? Ramshackle walls, grains scattered among burnt corpses, ashes carried away by the wind from burnt roofs, clothes, and currency notes saved up in pots... even the grinding stone had cracked from the heat!

Dogs had rambled around howling. Darkness had engulfed the uninhabited huts. In a street with a hundred houses, the wind had somehow 'carried' the fire and showered it on the houses of all but those who were in the good books of the landlords. Hot, ash-laden winds had swept through the empty streets. Burnt flesh had lain in molten clumps here and there. The goats and chickens that had not been tied up or confined had survived. They had wandered in the streets, bleating and clucking, around their burnt family members.

The authorities recorded it as an accidental fire. Even the newspapers reflected that view. Fearing for their lives, half the population moved to other places. They were so frightened that they did not even come back to receive the relief funds offered by the Government.

Every year, this rainy season tormented her by kindling the memories of not only her husband but also the decimation of the village.

Her *mama* rightfully visited her place often, claiming to visit his aunt. When neighbors enquired, he said, "Can't stay long without visiting aunt and uncle." He used to speak affectionately. What with his long sideburns, cat-fish-moustache and shiny black skin, she loved her *mama* a lot.

He belonged to a land in the west that saw very little rain. His uncle used to call him "the man from the west land." Uncle would also jokingly tick him off, calling him a "sister-fucker who eats *serukkal-millet*." With the freedom of a close relative and rights of a future father-in-law, his uncle rebuked him playfully, and sometimes reached a pitch. "How would those who catch field mice around the canal bunds appreciate our worth!" Her *mama* would also unrelentingly retaliate, saying, "Yeah, how would *we* appreciate the worth of *you* who knows nothing about relationships." The uncle would then crack the next whip at the right occasion. Realizing that it was risky to keep talking, her *mama* would slip away, saying, "I'll come again some other time." An incident that vindicated his uncle's words happened once. He had gone to call on his *chithappa* on his father's summons. When informed of the intent of his visit, the already-incensed wife yelled, "Go look for him at *Ambappura*'s house. He likes her juices better, you'll find him lying there!" She had burst out, unmindful of the words she was spilling in front of her nephew. It is common for a married woman to be called by the name of her husband's place when she visits her parents or comes to live with them after a separation. That is how he understood who *Ambappura* was. She was right; he had found his *chithappa* there. His aunt had resorted to such angry explosions because his *chithappa* treated the unrelated woman like his sister. Since *Ambappura* had lost her husband at a very young age in a caste riot and had settled alone there, the villagers did not think badly of this. As everyone in the village had some such story, they generally kept what they knew to themselves. Whenever some naughty youth of the village poked fun at him, the uncle, who was aware of these stories, would use one to shut them up. "Why wind him up and burn our butts"—youngsters in the village generally kept a safe distance from him.

Occasionally, his uncle also called him "the guy from the cashew plantations." True to the appellation, all along the way to his village, one could see cashew plantations on both sides of the narrow path. His birthplace was a rain-fed land and had now become a 'Government Forest' where millets, rye and ragi were cultivated in abundance.

They ploughed the field and cultivated groundnuts only when it rained. They would take sesame out of the seed box and scatter it across the field. Only those with the luxury of motor pumps and diesel engines would cultivate wetland crops like sugarcane, rice and bananas. People who worked in other towns were more than those who worked in fields. They had to live away from their families to be able to earn enough to meet their needs like food, clothing, and education. Those who did not wish to travel out of their town for work became either miscellaneous laborers, or coolies who do cattle work to domestic work, or did *vetti* work for their livelihood. Some went to nearby villages on daily wage work. Even though it was physically strenuous, since it did not pay, it is called *vetti* work, later earning a derogatory sense. Each *vetti* worker would serve more than five landlords. They would divide the houses they served such that each *vetti* worker got to serve around ten houses. If there was a death at a landlord's house, they were required to play the funeral drums during the last rites without pay. If there was a temple car festival, they are required to clean the streets along which the deity would pass. Before the use of electric lights, they would carry the heated Petromax lights on their heads all night long. Before Petromax, they carried firebrands for the temple car festivals and the *kuravan-kurathi* performances that went on until daybreak. Even now when there was electricity, the slum dwellers had to carry Petromax lights for extra lighting. They also 'served' the houses of the landlords assigned to each of them, doing everything from cutting firewood to filling water in the tank for cattle, in addition to being at the beck and call of the landlady. On new moon days, if they couldn't lay hands on lotus leaves, they had to collect leaves from portia trees, stitch them together with twigs, and deliver four or five such bunches to each house. They would also deliver firewood. At nightfall, the *vetti* worker, with his wife, would go to the same houses and call out 'Vettiyaanjaami' from outside the door. They would receive rice in their basket and gravy in a bowl before moving on to the next house. On festival days like Diwali and Pongal, a chicken and a packet of herbal shampoo would be added to the morning delivery, and in return, they received a dhoti-towel set and a few questionable *vadais*. At the end of the year, each *vetti* worker would get four bags of millet as compensation, which would mark the end of their contract with that landlord's family.

Even the farm laborers were not paid immediately after their work. After two or three days of waiting, the landlords would pay them with an air of doing them a favour. The labourers would walk all the way to the landlord's house every day to collect their pay. Each time, they would be given some work, and asked to come back the next day. The landlady's words drip with kindness only when she extracted work from these people.

One would never be able to tell apart the landlords from the labourers when they were seen defecating on the barren grounds with just their loin cloths on. Even though everything from their complexion to their build to their food habits was the same, the truth that they were all the same never dawned on the landlords. This race, which is ready to sacrifice even their lives to preserve the pride of their caste, kept the village and the slum apart. But the Government and religion regarded them collectively as 'Hindus.' And some men had taken it up as their primary occupation to brandish and assert these wretched beliefs.

When *vetti* workers returned with food in their baskets,

the youth on the street would tease them, asking, "*Mama*, did your landlady give you *vadai*?" Not realizing the reason behind the question, the worker would respond: "*Hm*.. Yes, she did." Then the youth would respond, "You ran all the way with your tongue hanging out only to get those stinking *vadais*?" The unsuspecting worker would only then realize the taunt. He would go home with the food, cursing under his breath, "Sister-fucker! Look how he teases me!"

These young men would impartially deride the landlords as well. There would be sexual slurs and expletives in their taunts and rebuke, making it unpleasant to the ears. Their scathing remarks would be along the lines of "it's sweet to extract work, but bitter to pay for it." One such funny incident happened to Mookkan's son. West Street's Mookkan's son had just finished college exams and had come home on his vacation. Only one or two youths from the slums went as far as to college. Bored at home, he went to meet his father at the landlord's house to get some money. At that moment, an altercation had been going on between the landlady and her daughter. Just as he was entering the landlord's house, the incensed mother had scolded her daughter, saying, "let a pariah fuck you!" This boy had immediately asked, "May I, *aayi*?" His friends still recall that and laugh whenever they see him. "The man from the west land", however, had never stepped into a landlord's place to work. He stopped studying after the tenth grade. Even in his schooldays, he would work only in the small land that belonged to his family. His father earned by cultivating groundnuts and pigeon peas. On days when there was no farming to be done, he would go to nearby villages to castrate cows and goats. If his father laid hands on them, even adamant bulls would mellow down and learn all tasks from ploughing to cart-pulling without the need for a neck rope. Goats, too, grew well after he castrated them, and went for high prices in the market. He was an expert at castrating not just cows and goats, but also dogs and pigs. Knowing his skills, the landlords in the village vied for his services. He would accept to castrate animals only for those who paid him something in advance. The villagers were envious of him as he never stooped to the level of a menial labourer.

"The man from the west land" frequently went to the town in search of jobs. His family had given up *vetti* work and the base act receiving alms even in his grandfather's time. People would occasionally call him for work, saying, "Your dad roams around with a castration tool all the time. At least you can come and do some work, right?" Saying "I have other business to attend to," he would shut their mouths. When his wedding was fixed, he went to the houses of the landlords to invite them for the wedding. Refusing to get the *aandaithaali* from the landlord, he raised the first ever objection to the tradition, which was a hot topic in the village for some time. This earned for his family the displeasure of the landlords.

During sowing time, he would go to his aunt's house to avoid getting into arguments with the villagers on taking up some work. He would return after cultivation, and go back again during the harvest. Whenever he, the nephew, came home, his aunt would prepare a feast and take him by surprise. She would make a different gravy every day, making the neighbors' mouths water even as it was cooking in the pot. His uncle would collect crabs, spearing them for the pot, and his aunt would make a spicy crab gravy. Another day, she would pick snails from the fields, break their shells, scoop out the flesh and fry it on a pan. Sometimes, the aroma from various delicacies ranging from field mice to storks to herons would invite neighbours looking for free curry.

On one such occasion, when he had come to Vazharaikurichi to buy chilli seedlings, he visited to see his aunt's daughter. His aunt's mother-in-law informed him that the couple had gone for work. Asking him to freshen up, have food and relax, she went to work at her landlord's place. The lizard in the house that was used to his frequent visits chirped at him teasingly. "How did I forget to ask where *she* has gone!" he wondered and waited for her longingly. When she came in with dripping hair, she enthusiastically asked after him, and entered the inner room to change into fresh clothes. She took out a saree from a pot and draped it. The fact that her *mama* was waiting outside the room made her timid and excited at the same time. She felt shy looking at her own body. The scent of the naphthalene balls that fell from her saree drifted across the house. Her turmeric-stained face shone brightly even in the dimly-lit hut. She brushed aside a strand of hair from across her forehead and stroked the mole at the corner of her lip. She was excited both in body and mind, and smiled unconsciously. "Please wait a little, *mama*. I'll prepare food…" As she went into the kitchen saying this, he grabbed her by her arm. "Let go of me, *mama*. Let me go, I say…" His hold only tightened.

His breath washed over her like hungry flames. "Let's not do anything before the wedding, *mama*…" She was shivering, and her voice trailed off weakly. She loved him a lot, but she was also afraid that something untoward may happen. Her feelings took over and her lower body started melting despite her resolve. Worried that things might get out of hand if she stayed quiet any longer, she cracked the 'whip.' "*Chi*, let go of me! Aren't you, after all, from the clan that mates with your own sisters!" Shocked, he withdrew as if someone had violently grabbed his balls. He went outside the house. A streak of pain tore through his heart. He was sweating profusely despite the rainy weather. He sat on the porch to get some fresh air. His teary eyes searched for something in the black clouds floating above. He was stunned, with embarrassment and remorse taking turns to whip him. He realized how brutishly and inappropriately he had behaved. She was indeed his aunt's daughter, and she was eventually to be married to him; but, he was disgusted with himself that he had forced it on her without her consent.

She talked to him cheerfully, without any inhibition. Moreover, she shared coarse riddles with him. Be that as it may, he should not have presumed that she was naturally attracted to him. Guilt was eating him from within. He sat cursing himself and wondered how he would placate her.

Anxious that her *mama* would leave, she sat beside him, took his finger and stroked it. "Are you mad at me, *mama*?" "Mm? No, rather pleased…" "Please don't be cross with me, *mama*. *Appayi* has told me not to get involved in anything of this sort before we are married. She also told me that the man I'm going to marry may leave me if did not heed her words. That's why I spoke that way, *mama*" "You still behave as if you know nothing about the world! I'm your intended, and we're going to be married in two months. Is this such an abominable sin? Or does this not happen anywhere else around us? Why do you point fingers at *Appayi*? The whole world knows that I'm going to marry you. Why fear then? Fear, she says!" She shyly buried her face on his shoulder. Uttering nothing more, he hugged her close and took her into the house. Not having experienced the proximity of a man before, she trembled. Beads of perspiration broke out on her face despite the drizzly breeze. The cat that had found shelter on the beam sprang down and ran away when they came in. The scent of old paddy from the clay drum had filled the entire house. The fierce wind carried the rain and sprayed it. Inside the house, too.

As she had wished, their wedding took place two months after that. Just when everything seemed to be flowing seamlessly in her life, the Panchayat election came up. Although it was a 'reserve' one, only the slum-dweller chosen by the village chief had so far held the post. That person would simply be a rubber stamp, while the actual post would be enjoyed by the chief or his brother. It is only when authorities visited the village that the chosen slum-dweller would have the opportunity to pose as the panchayat leader. In summary, it was the chief who served as the unelected leader at all times. Seeking a change in this long-held tradition, and wanting his people to enjoy the few rights the government had given them, and encouraged by his friends, her *mama* paid the deposit to contest in the panchayat election. The efforts of his parents and his villagers to stop (and protect) him went in vain. The landlord sent one man after another asking him to withdraw his nomination, but he stood firm and refused to budge. Deciding that it was impossible to convince him, the landlord sent some men to abduct him. They didn't know that he had gone to Jeyankondam with his friends to print posters for the election campaign.

Well-built and rather drunk, they entered the slum, broke open the cane gate and set foot in the house. Fearing something like this might happen, Nallathai had left her daughter-in-law and grandson at her brother's home in West Street. It turned out to be a good move. His father had hoped to fall at the feet of the henchmen and somehow pacify them, but now, watching the brutes enter the house, he thought: "What a blunder I've made! I should not have stayed back! *Pachaiyaayi*, please save us!" For the first time in his life, he was terribly afraid. The men tossed the coir cot out of the house. When the barking dog that sprung at them was thumped with a wooden log on its spine, it retreated to the streets, howling in pain. Shivering all over, his father fell at the feet of the henchmen. Since the man they had come for was not to be found, their rage descended on the old man. Their rough legs and hungry logs found their outlet on the old man. Failing in her feeble efforts at trying to save her husband, the old, emaciated woman fell on her husband's body and cried. Her cries grew louder and built up into a dirge, moistening even the pitch darkness outside.

Her voice saddened the people who stood behind the cacti and watched. The neighbors who call themselves kith and kin to each other rushed to the house with kerosene lanterns as soon as the henchmen had left.

"This is what happens when you stand against the landlord."

"Why do low-castes like us need posts and laurels!"

"Fool! Why wish to contest in the damned election and why bring agony to his parents!"

"What couldn't be disciplined at home has been disciplined by the village"

The villagers stood lambasting them. The old man bled to death. The daughter-in-law came carrying her infant. Seeing her dead father-in-law, she burst into tears. Aggravated by the chaos and clamour around, the baby started bawling. Woken by the cries of the women, the entire street gathered in front of the house.

When he returned home after midnight with posters in hand, he was shocked to see the crowd gathered in front of the house. Drawing closer, he noticed his wife and his family crying. As he realized what must have transpired, his eyes fell on his father's lifeless figure. With anger and grief flooding inside him, he held his father's feet and burst into loud tears.

It had been three days since the old man was cremated in the grounds to the south of the village. He made a decision on the fourth day. Leaving the cattle and the house in the care of his *chithappa*, he took his mother, wife and child to his aunt's place—his uncle and aunt had also come for the funeral. Despite its broken backbone, his dog dragged its body along the streets and came as far as the outskirts of the village to see him off. Looking at his dog, he felt rage welling up more than sorrow, spurring him to exact revenge. When tears brimmed in his eyes despite his restraint, he managed to swallow his pain and walked on.

Even at his aunt's place, he could stay put only for a couple of days. The enraged mind kept asking him when he was going to take action, fanning the embers that were ready to burst into flames anytime.

His resolve to take revenge before the Eighth Day following his father's death was getting stronger. The Homoeopathy doctor was the one who had lent him money for nomination and election expenses, and he was the one who had paid for father's funeral as well. It was on his advice that he had put off the idea of killing the landlord right away. Dr. Shahul Hameed and his father had been childhood friends. He had distributed the money given by the doctor among his friends and had given them clear instructions on when and where he would meet them. He called his wife. "Tell aunt that I'm going to the town." She pleaded with him not to go, but he silently left the house, determined. He ran his fingers across his waist—there was a bulge in his belt where a dagger lay sheathed.

His father's memories kindled his grief and rage. During the bus ride, he was grim as a machine incapable of social interaction. He got off the bus and walked half a mile through the cashew forest. Two figures emerged from behind a bush.

The duo had been waiting exactly where he had asked them to wait. Since it was close to full moon, the skies were grey, and one could see only a few stars scattered here and there. The sight of his friends gave him courage. His father's demise also squeezed his heart. They spread out and walked on. His resolve and courage hastened his stride. The sharpened dagger was ready in its leather sheath. Since there were defecating grounds behind the village chief's house, they walked through the eucalyptus grove. He asked his two friends to hide in a tamarind tree's shade, and proceeded cautiously, hiding behind the mango trees at the back of the house. He had already made it clear to his friends that their intervention would be needed only in case of a mishap. They therefore stayed ten feet behind. The landlord usually slept on a bench on the verandah. He felt anxious thinking about the task he had taken up. He knew he wouldn't get out alive if the slightest noise was heard. The village chief was asleep on the bench just as he had expected. His snores were ripping apart the silence of the night. He unsheathed the dagger and his fingers firmly gripped its handle. The thought of sweet revenge helped him keep his composure.

In one smooth slash, the sharp blade invaded the village chief's throat and tasted blood. His breath and his snores abruptly dissolved in the silent air. His mission accomplished, he sheathed the bloody weapon and quietly vacated the spot, leaving no signs; his receding footsteps on dead leaves made no rustle.

He informed his anxious friends of the successful execution and asked them to disperse, taking the narrow path going east. The two of them crossed the eucalyptus grove and hurried along that path. While the job they had come for was over, his anxiety had still not abated. He had to get past the cashew forest and reach the main road as soon as possible. He walked briskly, hoping to hitch a ride from the main road to the town police station, where he would surrender himself.

The call of the partridge bird was heard clearly. The full moon gradually appeared from behind the parting clouds. A fear had risen in him now: it was not fear for his life; it was the fear for the repercussions the slum would face. He had orchestrated a perfect revenge, but he wondered if he had acted without foresight. He didn't mind the consequences his action would have on his family. Now he became anxious that the ramifications would be far-reaching, affecting his people wherever the landlord's clan had the upper hand.

* * *

Rain was pelting down outside. Her son was collecting the water dripping from the roof in his palms. She pulled him and made him sit on her lap. Whenever her three-year-old son pointed at the picture of his father and asked about him in his child's voice, she felt a rage despite her gloom—like the red cucumis fruit that stands out even in the dense rain—and replied in an even voice: "Your father has gone to the jail, *pa.*" Gathering her innocent son to her chest, she began narrating the story of how his dad ended up in jail. The rain intensified. It was the rainy season, after all.

Glossary

serukkal-millet - a kind of millet
chithappa - father's younger brother
Ambappura - the woman of Ambapur
vetti work - a phrase referring to cutting wood and other odd jobs without pay, which has later come to mean 'useless work'
vadai - fritter
aandaithaali - ceremonial wedding badge given by landlords on the occasion of a wedding in the labourer's family

EARDRUM

AZHAGIYA PERIYAVAN

A big sturdy male buffalo had been slaughtered on the Mariamman Feast day, and now its hide has been cleaned and spread out to dry. A pit was dug behind the house and filled with pebbles, and the hide was soaked till all the hair came off. Then the softened hide was soaked some more. With gall-nut, babul tree bark and *aavaaram* bark added in the proper proportions, it was given even more soaking. Any hair which was still clinging to the hide was then scraped away with a sharp knife, and the hide was stretched and pegged down firmly at the four corners. He had set it out in the sun to dry and kept vigil near it lest the dogs drag it away. Everything was ready. Today was the day when it had to be made. This time too, the search for wood from a jackfruit tree had turned out to be very frustrating. *Thanakkan* wood was available, but that was not what he used.

Translated by Malini Seshadri
Original Source: 'Sevipparai', *Theettu*, Chennai: Tamizhini, 2000
English Translation: *The Oxford India Anthology of Tamil Dalit Writing* edited by Ravikumar & R Azhagarasan (OUP, 2012)

Except Chinnakuzhandai, there was not a single soul in that village who knew how to make a *thappu*. He would grip the hide firmly, twist it and tie it down, and then each blow on the drum leather would bring forth a booming response. He had grown old now, but he had not lost his ability.

Kaatturaja arrived early in the morning.

'*Yov, Maama*. Come on, get up. Let's go. We have to finish the job today.'

Kaatturaja, Chinnakuzhandai and Saaman went to Kupputhaayi's house, downed some arrack, and then went to the cattle-shed in Kaatturaja's yard. Kaatturaja had brought with him some meat that he had asked his wife to cook. The pungent smell of cattle urine was in the air. The work got under way on the manure-smeared floor of the cattle-shed. A pot and a drum-frame hung side by side in a corner.

Chinnakuzhandai cut the leather hide to the size of the frame and started making holes in it at regular intervals of a handspan. Kaatturaja tore strips of leather from the leftover hide. The sour smell of gall-nut in which the hide had soaked rose in waves from the leather. They first pulled the leather over the frame and tied down all four corners firmly. Then they carefully threaded the leather thongs through the holes, twisted them and tied them tight.

'How the times have changed, *raja*! Nowadays they are using plastic sheets and screw bolts to make drums. Their drums make a dup…dup sound. Now this is what I call a *real* drum. When you beat it, see how it vibrates… DUNG…DUNG.'

'Oh, don't talk about all that. Why don't you sing that *uri*[1] song?'

Uriyo uri uriyo uri
Panaimarathila paachhai
Ungamma..nda dosai
Uriyo uri uriyo uri
Marakkaa saama aalu
Marakka pillai pethaan
Uriyo uri uriyo uri.
Uriyo uri uriyo uri
Cockroach on the palm tree
Your Amma's cunt is like a dosa
The fellow with the big thing
Has fathered a big son
Uriyo uri

Saaman and Kaatturaja rolled in mirth, their stained teeth on view.

'*Maama*, they are showing a damn good movie in Kalaimagal Cinema House. What dancing that actress Silk does, swaying her buttocks and all! You would never have seen such a thing in your time. Let's go this evening.'

'Even at this age the fellow just loves to see those Silk movies. He will go and sit in the front row, and whenever her dance scene comes he will bend close to the floor and try to peer up her skirt.'

---

1 In this context, an uri is a pouch made with palm leaves and a long thread and filled with firecrackers. It is used as a firecracker in festivals.

Saaman and Kaatturaja burst out laughing again. Chinnakuzhandai was paying no attention to them and was concentrating on tightening the drum thongs. He was rather hard of hearing. He was totally deaf in one ear, and could hear only slightly in the other. One had to go right up to him and shout into his ear. The children of the village would come near him as though wanting to tell him something, and then they would shout 'Coo' into his ear and run away. Even the grown-ups would humiliate him. They would make rude remarks and laugh mockingly.

Now the *thappu* was ready. Chinnakuzhandai derived great joy in stroking and handling it. It was as if the feel of the drum in his hand gave his whole arm a new burst of joyful energy. By sheer force of habit he started playing the *thappu*. Chinnakuzhandai was in a class by himself when it came to playing the *thappu*. No one could match him in this. He was the master of all kinds of solo drum playing. *Othadi, ottiyadi, alangaram, thullal, tangu*...his fingers could play any or all of the sounds and rhythms. There had been a time when Chinnakuzhandai was the drummer everyone wanted, for every occasion and every festival... weddings and funerals, religious festivals and processions, coming-of-age and ear-piercing ceremonies. Those days were gone. Nowadays people had started engaging bands for all the occasions. Chinnakuzhandai was still banging away ferociously on the newly made drum. His mind too was vibrating with the drum. His eyes grew bright and glistened. His face muscles were stretched and his teeth were visible. His hands, his whole body, the music itself...

everything pulsated. The very air reverberated with the sound; the cattle-shed, the house, the street itself seemed to leap and twitch with the sound. So fiercely did he beat that drum that every stroke of his hand was a booming call to break into dance…and to keep dancing till every nerve and blood vessel in the body was strained to breaking point. Indeed, Kaatturaja had started dancing.

It had been a long time since Chinnakuzhandai had played on a *thappu.* In earlier days, for every occasion, someone would come and fetch Chinnakuzhandai and his *thappu.* Once his son had grown and taken up a government job, Chinnakuzhandai had stopped accepting those invitations. His son too had made his feelings very clear.

'Do you want me to move around in this village with dignity or not? If you go around playing drums any more, I will be really furious.'

If only he could once again play the drum to accompany old Parvathy's song….

O you whose perfume pervades the world
O you elegant doe-like maiden,
O my adorable one
On whom the lovely five-hued parrot is perched
O truly a princess you are…

Once Parvathy got going, she could keep singing till the fingers of the drummers grew tired of playing. She could produce an endless stream of songs. Songs for the fields, *kummi* songs, lullabies, dirges, all these were in Parvathy's repertoire. Those were the days when Chinnakuzhandai could still hear well. They had been ploughing Arsad Bai's fields which they had taken on lease. Each day was a joy, steeped in the sweet nectar of blossoming flowers. Even to this day the old man would insist that it was only in response to her singing that the crops in the field flourished so well. It was also around that time that Arsad Bai installed a water-pump in the field. No one in and around the village had ever owned a water-pump like this. The miracle of water gushing out of a pipe at the mere press of a button! Chinnakuzhandai had the childish habit of putting his ear to the end of the water-pipe to listen to the echoing sounds inside. The sounds were somewhat like the ones from telegraph cables. One day, when Chinnakuzhandai had his ear pressed to the opening of the pipe, Parvathy pressed the button. The force of the gushing water flung Chinnakuzhandai away to a distance. He fell against a tree and a sharp twig from it entered his ear and ruptured the eardrum. He became deaf in that ear. The force with which the water had slammed against his head had affected the hearing in the other ear too. From that day onwards, Parvathy stopped singing altogether.

Chinnakuzhandai watched two movies every week. Rain or shine, he would go. He would buy a ticket for a floor seat, settle down on a pile of sand and, munching from a packet of gram, watch the show. As for today's movie, Kaatturaja had told him that Silk was in it, but that was a lie. Chinnakuzhandai's anger against Kaatturaja and Saaman for this deception was soon assuaged by the actress Meena. By the time the film was drawing to an end, his mind had no room for any thought except Meena. Is there any movie in which the hero is a *thappu* player? In all these years of watching films, he had never come across a single one with a hero like that. The old man's mind became troubled. Even as the movie was going on, during a change of scene, Chinnakuzhandai's mind drifted away and lost touch with reality. With his dhoti tucked up, Bharathi is scattering the seedlings in the fields. The planting is going on in full swing. The young women have their sarees tucked up above their cucumber thighs. Beautiful Kannammal steps forward and bursts into song. Her music swells, wave upon wave, and captivates Bharathi. Chinnakuzhandai felt a pleasurable thrill. After all, Parvathy was about the same age as Meena, wasn't she? Vigour and vitality coursed through the old man.

That night he had a dream. Never in his life had he ever had a dream like this one. Everything in the world was made of drums. The sky was a gigantic drum, and so was the earth below. The ground that reverberated to the sound of running or walking footsteps was a drum. The moon was a drum. Everywhere, drums and more drums. Chinnakuzhandai is wandering around searching among the drums for Parvathy. His every breath, his merest touch make the drums resound, and the waves of drum-beats pursue him. After he has run a long way, he comes to an open valley. Once his eyes adjust to the dim light, he can see that the place is filled with *koel** birds. Parvathy is there, with *koels* resting on her shoulders and arms. He takes the moon-drum out of the sky. They both climb and climb till they reach the very top of a mountain. She sings. He plays the drum. The whole valley is their music. The sky fills up with it and the song-drops rain down in a musical downpour. The dream was still gnawing at his mind the next morning as Chinnakuzhandai set off before dawn to buy arrack. No children or grandchildren at home. Utter solitude. As the two of them sat down with a bowlful of curry, and between them finished off the contents of the arrack bottle, Chinnakuzhandai and Parvathy could sense the rotation of the earth. Like puffs of cotton wool they were floating in the breeze. The old man started praising Meena. Parvathy went into a sulk. Overcome with emotions he had never experienced before, the old man embraced Parvathy and tried to kiss her…and received a slap on his face. He begged her to sing. He entreated and cajoled. The old woman obstinately refused.

The previous week the old man had gone to meet his son who lived in another town. He had asked him for a hearing aid.

'What's the need for it at this age?'

'Even your mother makes fun of me, *da*. I can't bear the way the whole village teases me.'

Just to keep his father satisfied the son took him on a so-called visit to a doctor. 'When I come next month I'll bring the hearing aid, *appa*,' he said, and sent the old man home.

One day at dawn, when the light was still murky, Parvathy dashed the old man's fondest hopes to ashes. The old woman died. A heavy feeling descended on Chinnakuzhandai's chest. It was the weight of grief. It was a weight that would not allow him to think of anything, decide anything, do anything. He could not accept the fact that she was gone. Neither could he weep. Again and again, he would come and stand near her body and stare at her with wild eyes and then go away to sit in some corner. Kaatturaja and Saaman took him away and filled him to the brim with arrack. He mumbled and muttered incoherently. In fact, the house of death seemed to be a place of peace for the old man. People were talking all around him. But he heard nothing. Relatives and groups of village women clustered in groups and sobbed. He did not hear them. In front of the house, Kaatturaja and Saaman were playing the drums. He did not hear that either.

He imagined that people were paying their respects to Parvathy in deep silence. He imagined that in a soundless world Parvathy had been laid out on view for everyone to come and gaze upon. Or, could it be that it was Parvathy who had snatched away all sound from everywhere and was refusing to let it go, wondered the old man. All kinds of people came and went. But not his son. A messenger had been sent to fetch him.

Though his son had been inviting them to come and stay with him, the old man and woman had decided to stay on in the village all these years. Parvathy was the one who had been there for him. Now she was gone. Hereafter, even the old man's life was uncertain. It was a question of when the end would come. Everyone was talking…the old woman won't abandon him, they were saying, she will take him with her….so many words piling up and sliding around.

The sons of the landowner whose fields Chinnakuzhandai

had tilled came and paid their respects. Memories flooded through the old man's mind. His eyes clouded over, and he collapsed in a deep faint.

There was a big commotion. They took him into the house and put him in a chair. He regained consciousness and came outside again. The crowd swelled. The people moved about as if they had forgotten there was a corpse in their midst. The bundles of incense sticks wafted their essence in swathes of smoke. In the midst of it all lay the old woman, like a dry twig.

Her mouth was open. She looks as if she is lying there singing; maybe she is singing right now; it is just that I can't hear her, the old man told himself. It struck him with full force for the first time that he was deaf. So many years had gone by without his being able to hear her speak or sing. His whole existence had come to depend on sign language or words shouted close to his ear. As he churned these thoughts over in his mind, something seemed to dissolve deep within his consciousness. His son arrived.

New sounds of wailing and sobbing arose in the house of death. The old man too could no longer stop himself from weeping. The tears streamed from his eyes.

Once Parvathy had been buried and everyone had gone home, the house seemed very empty. He could not bring himself to go on living there alone. Unable to bear the restless fever of loneliness, he set out for Kaatturaja's house. Presently, the enticing sound of the drum began to send out its invitation. Chinnakuzhandai's fingers had found their rhythm. Kaatturaja appeared from somewhere. 'Maama, what is happening?' he asked in astonishment.

'Your aunt is singing, *da*.'

After a pause, the *thappu's* steady beat started up again.

Glossary

aavaram: a type of tree.
thanakkan: a type of tree from which drums are sometimes made.
thappu: drum made of a wooden frame with animal hide stretched across it.
kummi: Dance, usually by young women, involving coordinated steps and hand-clapping, to the accompaniment of a rhythmic song. They dance in a circle around a pot placed in the centre of a colourful decorated pattern on the floor.
koel: A kind of cuckoo bird

PALLA STREET

VIZHI PA IDHAYAVENDHAN

***Editor's Note:** The story brings out the rigid caste hierarchy in villages, where streets are named after the castes who live on them. There is little or no socializing between caste groups and intermarriage is taboo. People of the same caste differ in their outlook and aspirations depending on whether they live in a city slum or in a village. The Chakkiliyars and Parayars are 'depressed castes' whereas the Udayars and Mudaliars are 'higher castes'. The social, financial and power profiles of the different castes also mirror the same hierarchy.*

Chakkili Street was an island unto itself. Like something chewed dry and spat out ....that was the kind of existence here. With no one to turn to, each had to struggle alone for survival.

The street was at the northern border of the town, where the ground sloped downwards. In time it came to be known as Palla Street, a play on the word 'Palla' which means 'low'

Translated by Malini Seshadri
Original Source: *Dalit Sirukathai Thoguppu:* An Anthology of Dalit Short Stories compiled by P Sivakami (Sahitya Akademi, 2014)

as well as being the name of a Dalit caste. Inside the town itself was a slum that, in the course of time, came to be called 'Periya Colony'. There too there were Parayars and Chakkiliyars. But those Parayars had nothing in common with the Chakkiliyars of Palla Street. Indeed, it would be difficult to find anything in common between even the Chakkiliyars in the town and those on Palla Street.

The Chakkiliyars of Palla Street could not lay claim to any special benefits based on their caste identity. It was the accepted norm that the Chakkiliyars in the town slum were subservient to the Parayars there; but it was also accepted that they were superior to the Chakkiliyars on Palla Street, making the latter the bottom of the heap. Although all these were under the common umbrella of 'depressed castes' as far as the District administration was concerned, there was an unspoken hierarchy that operated among them.

It was not that the Chakkiliyars of Palla Street were people of a different kind. It was only through the nature of their work that they were differentiated, like the differences between the fingers of a hand. There were labourers and rickshaw pullers, fruit sellers and petty shop owners, musicians for funerals and for auspicious occasions. A few worked in government offices. The Chakkiliyars who lived inside the town had their hutments on Nandanar Street. They too did pretty much the same kinds of work that the ones of Palla Street did. In addition, many were cobblers.

To outward appearances, the Chakkiliyars of Nandanar Street seemed prosperous enough. Despite their grinding poverty, the total lack of schooling for the children, and having hardly a cooking vessel at home, they were fond of wearing sparkling clean and smart looking clothes. Even as they enjoyed some of the advantages that town life gave them, they had an unrealistic urge to aspire to a matching lifestyle. Social acceptance was essential in order to avoid being discriminated against; and so the kinds of work they had to do to earn their livelihood caused them conflict and anguish.

There was nothing in common and no kind of communication between the Chakkiliyars of Nandanar Street and those of Palla Street. Even when they chanced to meet, the contemptuous expressions on their faces, like mustard spluttering in smoking oil, conveyed mutual animosity. Tempers would flare; mocking, scathing words would be exchanged. This was the divide that 'town culture' had brought about. It was impossible to even think about offering or accepting daughters in marriage between families of the two streets. If such a relationship were to develop the couple would have to flee or run the risk of being killed.

So the Palla Street Chakkiliyars, like castaways on an island, with no identity, no address and no support from anywhere, existed on the edge, dangling precariously on the periphery of the town. Very often the Street leader Rangasamy expressed his anguish: 'What sin did we commit to be consigned to this wretched existence!'

Yet Rangasamy's grievance was not totally reasonable. Most of the people of Palla Street did 'unclean' manual jobs in the town, as scavengers, cleaners of drains, sewage pipes and septic tanks, repairers of carts, and disposers of unclaimed corpses. Not a single one had a job requiring an education. Yet, there were now a few who were studying.

It was the nature of the work done to earn a livelihood that sets people apart from one another, even within the same caste. Unable to join hands and move forwards with the sentiment 'I am a human being and so are you', they are unable to escape the discrimination that the town culture has ordained.

The national highway ran at a higher level above Palla Street. Across it was a railway crossing gate. Two kilometres beyond this was the limit for any kind of regular work activity related to the town. After that, just wide open spaces with nothing stirring. Someone could get beaten up in the open here, and no one would know. At the edges of the smooth tarred highway were a few tiny kiosks and eateries.

The town itself had grown and expanded. A Mariamman temple, a Perumal temple, a Siva temple, houses, schools, jewellery stores, clothing stores, and vegetable shops had come up. On the side opposite to Palla Street, to the west, on the road to Viraatikuppam, some young boys had set up country liquor shops. Further away was the office of a political party...or maybe it was a fan club for a movie star.. depending on whom one asked.

The streets closest to the highway contained, for the most part, the houses of those belonging to higher castes. Udayars and Mudaliars had purchased much of the land just beyond the railway crossing. In the interior areas of Muthampalayam, at the borders of the lake, were flourishing sugarcane fields which added continuously to the wealth of their owners.

Many of the sons of these landlords, born into a life of luxury, may or may not have been getting an education. But they certainly spent a lot of time drinking and hanging around idly with their friends, and creating trouble. These gangs of boys...Chinnapayyan, Mohan, Das, Ibrahim, Selvaraj, Kumar and their like....grew into adulthood just roaming around aimlessly.

The Palla Street people kept well clear of the higher-caste fellows and avoided confrontations of any kind. At the end of the working day, they would return exhausted, almost to the point of collapse. Then some of them would set out with bottle or bag to buy some oil or rice. Others would go to fetch a jug of tea. And some would go to Ibrahim's liquor shop to drink a glass and return quietly.

One evening, Kadirvelu went to Ibrahim's shop to buy liquor. The shop was in narrow track lined with thorn bushes.

'De, how much do you want?' Ibrahim demanded.

'I want a whole jug full. Will you give it to me?' was Kadirvelu's response, accompanied by a laugh.

'How much money do you have?'

'Five rupees.'

Ibrahim stood up and slapped Kadirvelu hard across the face.

'What impertinence! So you want a whole jug of liquor for just five rupees?'

'*Ayyayyo*! I said it as a joke, Anna. Please don't be angry.'

Ibrahim lashed out and kicked him.

'I'm worn out to the bone with slaving all day. Don't kick me like that, Anna. My whole body is sore.'

As Ibrahim continued to kick Kadirvelu mercilessly, the other customers who were enjoying their liquor and meat snacks at the shop were laughing in enjoyment of the spectacle. Ibrahim rolled Kadirvelu around in the mud. Covered with grime and slush and caked with sweat and dust, Kadirvelu got to his feet and tried to shake off some of the muck.

'Show me your money,' demanded Ibrahim. Kadirvelu stared back at him in silence.

'How dare you glare at me like that!'

'I don't want the liquor.'

'Why don't you want it?'

'Why should I take a kicking from you and also buy your liquor? What's your age and what's mine? Yet you raised your hand against me. I'll go a little further and buy my liquor at our *cheri*.'

Ibrahim became even angrier. He grabbed Kadirvelu by his shirt and shook him violently. The couple of buttons that had still been attached to the shirt flew off. Ibrahim clenched his teeth in fury.

'Anna, leave me alone. I can't take this kind of beating. Here's five rupees. Give me whatever you wish to.'

He could not get high on the liquor. He came home staggering and sore from the beating.

It was the general impression among the higher caste folk that the Palla Street people were simpletons. That was why even fellows in their teens had no regard for age or seniority when they used disrespectful terms like '*va da, po da*' or '*va di, po di*' to the Palla Street folk. Swear words and abuses were also plentiful. As though they had their own private *panchayat* with its own rules, the youngsters of the higher castes often came up with some reason or other to physically attack, intimidate or take away money from the Palla Street residents.

Here on Palla Street there was no common sense of purpose to offer a united resistance to oppression, no common strategy devised for everyone to follow. It was not so with the youngsters of the higher castes. Every kind of misadventure and outrage was supported and endorsed by the elders of the caste. Even if the police were brought in, the culprits would be home again soon with the support of the authorities. This was why the youngsters never feared the consequences of their actions.

That evening, on Palla Street, a bitter quarrel broke out between Natarajan and his wife Kamala. It was very late when she came home to cook the night meal. She had gone to meet the money lender who had promised to give her some money that day. She waited till seven but he never turned up. She went home empty-handed.

'Which fellow were you with for such a long time, di?'

'I only went to meet the money lender. But he didn't come.'

'Were you standing there all the time?'

'What else? You think I was lying on my back? Get lost, you drunkard!'

The quarrel escalated into a stormy exchange of words.

Then he hit her and dragged her on to the street. He shouted, 'I don't want to live with you any longer. Go away!' Kamala wailed loudly.

As though to add fuel to this raging fire, it so happened that Chinnappayyan, one of the higher caste youth, was standing outside an eatery nearby. The loud cries of Kamala fell upon his ears and lent wings to his feet. He rushed up to them and landed a couple of resounding slaps on both of them.

Natarajan whined, 'Sami, you tell me. The children are left hungry while she roams around the place and turns up so late.'

'Enda, so you think she's a low-life like you?'

The incident was long over. Natarajan was moaning in excruciating pain. The children had gone to sleep with their hands clutching his legs. As word of the happenings spread, people grew indignant. Manichandran, Perumal and others went as a group to the *naatamai* and related what had happened. The old man was overcome with sorrow.

'What do you want me to do?' he asked them. Everyone had something to say.

'How can we allow this sort of thing to go on?'

'But can we survive if we antagonize those people.'

'We are not dependent on them for anything. We earn our living by working.'

'That sounds brave, but....'

'Look, they will keep coming back here fully drunk. For no reason at all they will beat up somebody. How long can we stand by and do nothing?'

'It's becoming a habit with them.'

'We shouldn't go on tolerating this. Why should those fellows interfere in our street's affairs? Come, let us go to the police.'

When he heard mention of the police, *naatamai* Rangasamy couldn't help laughing aloud even in the midst of his sombre mood. The fact was, whatever problems arose on Palla Street went no further. Like halwa falling into the hands of rowdy elements, no one would talk about it. Even if the Chakkiliyars inside the town came to hear about the atrocities happening here, they would just ignore them. Now, as he finished laughing, the naatamai reminded them of this reality. Turning towards Manian, he said,

'Let's not buy trouble, pa.'

Again a chorus of protests arose.

'Oh, so you are telling us to go on taking their beating and kicking.'

'All of us, all fifty families are abandoned orphans.'

'No, no, not orphans, we work for the government don't we?'

'Ha, this same government's police fellows are the ones who applaud and laugh mockingly whenever we take a complaint to them.'

'If we do nothing about this, we would lose every last shred of our respectability.'

'Which of us on the street has any respectability right now anyway?' remarked the *naataamai*.

'*Naatamai* saar, please don't devalue our own people. We are equal to anyone else. It's only because our living standards are so low that you think of talking this way. We are not to blame for our plight. The blame lies with the one who rules us, who grows wealthy by cheating us. Realise that. Don't go on living in the past.'

'De, how grandly you all speak. If you had actually learnt how to read and write a couple of words....then where would you be?'

'Look, are you coming with us or not?'

'Even in an emergency one must be cautious, da.'

Perumal rebuked the *naatamai.*

'Enna, Annae, enough of this idle chatter.'

All eyes turned to Perumal. Meanwhile, hearing loud arguments going on at the *naataamai*'s house, a curious crowd had gathered.

'Remember what happened the other day. Because our Kanchana would not go and dance at one of their funerals, that Das fellow came and beat her up and broke all her kitchen vessels. None of us said or did anything. Kanchana dances for fun on our street. Does it mean it is her fate to dance at their funerals? Then there was the time when he grabbed Rukmani by the hand, dragged her towards him and embraced her. One day he does this in a state of drunkenness.... another day he may take her to his bed. That Mohan fellow is no better. He couldn't win in a fair game of cards. He lost to Ettikottai of all people, and later beat him up and forced him to give the money back. As for Ibrahim, he comes around on the day our wages get paid, presents false bills for liquor and extorts money. In that matter of trying to get compensation from the government for a death, this Selvaraj fellow passed himself off as the cousin or brother-in-law or something of Ponnusamy and took away all the money. If each of those fellows goes on behaving this way, what's to be done? Have we given them some written undertaking that we will be their slaves for ever?'

Pattammal Paati nodded in agreement with Perumal. In the deepening darkness, Perumal posed his question again. '*Naatamai* saar, will you come?'

The *naatamai* raised his bowed head. 'If it is to the police, I am not coming.'

'All right, at least come with us to Sundaram Udayar's house.'

'What?...To our Councillor's house?'

'Yes.'

'Why?'

'Ha, what do you think? For you both to exchange *tamboolams**? What a silly question. Do you remember how our Natarajan was beaten up so badly that he won't be able to move about for ten or fifteen days? Did you know it was Udayar's son Chinnapayyan who did that?'

'Don't you fellows know about Udayar?' asked the *naataamai.*

'What...that he buys votes to win elections?'

'He threatens to beat us up if we don't vote for him. If we protest he says he will burn down our houses,' explained the *naatamai.*

'Oh, all right. This fellow is obviously not coming with us. Let us get going, da.'

A small group of them set off for Sundaram Udayar's house. He was surrounded by a group of his party men.

One of them alerted him, 'Anna, the Chakkili fellows have come.'

Udayar stepped outside. When the Palla Street delegation told him about what his son had done, he was quick to retort, 'Who can stand by and tolerate drunken brawling?'

'But does that justify such behaviour from your son?'

'De, what can you fellows do?'

'Don't talk to us like that.'

'Police...courts...I can take care of everything. Do you know that?'

'If that's so, we also know something about justice. The next time any of your fellows enters our street, we will do the talking.'

'Oh, you dare to throw a challenge at me, eh? Get lost, you dirty dogs!'

They returned to Palla Street, fuming and muttering under their breaths. Why did we ever go to such a fellow expecting any justice, they asked themselves. But some pointed out that it was just as well, because if anyone were to ask in the future if we had brought our grievance to the Councillor's notice, we can say yes, we did.

It was a Sunday. Some people were playing *pallaankuzhi* near Ponnusamy's house. In the front porch of Mani's home, a group was playing cards. Because it was a holiday, many were resting or sleeping in their houses or on the *thinnais* outside their front doors. A sudden commotion drew everyone's attention.

Das, one of the higher-caste youth, was entering the

street. He was very drunk. In one hand was a long knife. With the other he clutched at his lungi which had come loose. The women trembled in fear.

'Is there no one to stop this fellow?'

'Filthy dog! What a loafer of a son the father has produced.'

'The fellow is looking for trouble.'

More and more abuses rained down on him. Das came staggering along, holding on to his *lungi*. The card players paused and glared at him. Smoke curled up into the air from Mani's beedi. Das collapsed on the *thinnai* outside Rukmini's house and shouted, "Ey, Rukmini, where are you, di?'

The card players got up and approached. Das looked up at them drunkenly.

'Enna da, what are you doing here?' asked one of the men.

'How dare you call me '*da*'?' Das spluttered as he scrambled to his feet in indignation.

'Go away quietly,' they told him.

'What can you do to me? If you come near me I will carve you up with my knife. Take care.'

Mani's friends tried to restrain him. Don't create trouble, they said, let the fellow go. They started pulling him away.

'Why are you glaring at me, da?' taunted Das. 'Rukmini took fifty rupees from me and promised to sleep with me. Did you know that?'

'De, get lost now! Or else....' Mani shoved Das hard. The latter brandished his knife. The two of them got into a furious fight, rolling around in the mud on the street. Mani snatched away the knife and kicked Das in the face. Blood gushed out. Perumal broke a bottle of toilet-cleaner acid and raised it high in his other hand. Das recognised the danger of his position. He took to his heels and fled towards the west road.

'Yes, run, you filthy dog. We are not the ones who fear for our lives.'

Perumal's voice reached a crescendo. The acid that had spattered when he broke the bottle was raising painful blisters on his hands. The women came closer. They put their sari *pallus* around his hands and held them tight. The burning sensation grew into an excruciating pain which exploded in his head.

Glossary

Cheri: Slum settlement

Panchayat: Village council

Naataamai: Village headman

Thaamboolam: Plate or tray with offerings of fruit, etc.

Pallankuzhi: An old game played traditionally with shells and a board with shallow cups. A modern version in some countries is Mancala

Thinnai: A shaded verandah with a resting area at the front of a house

Lungi: Casual wrap-around lower garment for men

Pallu: The part of the sari draped over the shoulder

CONTRIBUTORS

Cho Dharuman

Cho Dharuman is a leading dalit writer, widely known as one of the *karisal* writers. He has published two novels *Thoorvai* and *Koogai* and a non-fiction work, *Villicai Vendar Pichakkutti*. His short story collections include *Eeram*, *Sogavanam*, *Vanakumaran*, and *Cho Dharuman Kathaikal*. He has received several awards including Best Short Story Writer of the Year awards in 1992 and again in 1994, the Katha award in 1993, the Tamil Nadu Government Award in 2007 and Ilakkiya Thottam award from Toronto University in 2008. Translations of his stories have appeared in several journals including *Indian Literature,* and in national dailies including *Indian Express, Economic Times* and *The Hindu*. His novel *Sool* won the Sahitya Akademi award in 2019.

Kovedha Swaminathan

Kovedha Swaminathan is a former Vice Principal of American College, Madurai. To date, he has published 22 books including poetry, short stories, novels, translations, and non-fiction books on folklore, culture, history, human rights and subaltern issues. After his retirement from service he lives in Madurai.

V Venkatachalam

V Venkatachalam is a short story writer and poet. His poems have appeared in the literary magazines, *Sundara Suthan, Kanavu, Sadangai, Verkal, Vannakkathi, Pudhiya Kodangi* and *Dalit.* His poetry collection, *Oli Pukaa En Azhagiya Veedu* appeared in 2002 and his short story collection, *Pachai Manasu* appeared in 2007.

Gowthama Sannah

Gowthama Sannah is a writer and ideologue of dalit politics and sociology. He has published over 80 articles in several Tamil magazines since 1995. He has also written several stories and books on dalit and social issues. His book, *Anti-Conversion Act - History, Socio-Political background and its Impact* was published in 2006 and *Panditharin Kodai* 2007. His other writings include *Kalakathin Maraiporul, Tamilan Ozitha Sathi,* and *Kurathiaru,* a mythical history and magical realistic account of the river Kotralai. Sannah is a dalit activist and member of the VCK political party. His activities include the formation of various sangams and federations to campaign for the rights of dalits.

Abimani

Abimani alias E. Mani has several short story collections to his credit including *Nookkadu, Paaram Sumappavarkal, Panai Muni, Thettam, Oorchoru, Matravarkal* and *Ethiraga.* He was honoured for his writings by the Bharathi MurpookkuVaalibarkal Sanga and Tiruppur Tamil Sangam.Hisstory. *Oorchoru* won the Kalki Memorial prize and the collection of stories under that same title won the Tamil Nadu Government award. The collection *Ethiraga* won an award from the MurpokkuEzhuthalar Sangam.

P Sivakami

P Sivakami is a writer and activist and an IAS official. She has written three novels, *Anandayee*, *Palayana Kazhidalum*, and *Kurukku Vettu*and *Pa Ka Aa Ku-Sila Kurippukal (1995)*, four collections of short stories besides a non-fiction work on feminism, *Udalarasiyal*. She has held very senior positions in various Tamil Nadu Government Departments. Through her *Dalit Nila UrimaiIyakkam*, she has raised awareness about land rights for dalit women. She has campaigned for reservation for dalits in the private sector and also for the rights of transgenders.

Imayam

Imayam alias V Annamalai, has published three novels - *Koveru Kaluthakal, Aarumugam* and *Sedal* and two short story collections, *Manparam* and *Video Mariamman*. His much acclaimed first novel *Koveru Kaluthakal* won awards from the Agni Aksara Trust, Tamil Nadu Progressive Writers' Forum in 1994, and Amudhan AdigalIlakkiya award for Literature in 1998. The English translation of this novel appeared under the title *Beasts of Burden*. Recently he received the award for Best Writer from the Government of Tamil Nadu. He has been a volunteer of the Dravida Munnetra Kazhagamparty for more than two decades.

Theynmozhi

Theynmozhi's collection of poems appeared as *Thuravi Nandu* in 2008 and her first collection of short stories appeared as *Nerkkunjam* publications in 2009. She played a key role in establishing the literary forum *Ilakkiya Cholai* in the Thanjavur region. She has compiled the creative writings of trans-genders under the title, *Maadavappilai.* Her short story collection *Koonalpirai* won an award in 2016. She was the recipient of the SPARROW award for 2019. She has completed her research on Art History at Thanjavur Tamil University.

Bama

Bama is a celebrated contemporary Dalit writer in Tamil. She has been in the forefront of feminist and anti caste literature activism and has given Dalit aesthetics tremendous visibility. Besides her path-breaking autobiographic novel *Karukku* (1992), her other works include *Sangati, Vanmam, Manushi, Kisumbukkaran, Oruthathhavumerumayum* and *Thavittukuruvi.* Her works have been translated into English, French and several regional languages. In 2001, the English translation of *Karukku* won the Crossword Prize establishing her as a distinct voice in Dalit literature. At present, she has written a novel titled *Virutchangalagum Vithaigal* which is ready for publication.

Ravikumar

Ravikumar is a poet, translator, biographer, columnist, rights activist and theorist of the Dalit movement in Tamil Nadu. He has edited more than 30 books and magazines. A collection of his writings appeared in English as *Venomous Touch.* He is a co-founder of the publishing house, Navayana. He served as Member of Legislative Assembly of Viduthalai Ciruthaikal Katchi during 2006 -11.

Pratibha Jeyachandran

This prolific writer's poetry and short stories have appeared in several Tamil magazines. His collection of stories appeared as *Puthahathilirundhu Purappatta Prathimaigal.* He prepared the script for the short film, *Ethirveechu*, which was directed by K Rangaraj. He was honoured with *Silpi Award for Literature.* He is a Resource Person for the Tamil Nadu Government's sensitisation programme for bureaucracy on the welfare of SC/STs.

Pablo Arivukkuyil

E. Arivazhagan writes under the name Pablo Arivukkuyil. His poetry has been regularly published in magazines like *Thaamarai, Deepam*, *Kanaiyazhi*, and *Nigazh.* He burst into the prose arena after winning the *Kanaiyazhi - ThiJanakiraman* short novel contest. As the first publication of Vilippu Trust, *Kilukki*, an anthology of his short stories, was published by Vidiyal publishers (Coimbatore) in 1995. He has five collections of short stories and a novel, *Thamugu,* to his name.

Azhakiya Periyavan

Azhakiya Periyavan alias C Aravindan, is known for his active participation in forums relating to education and dalit issues. He became a significant writer with his first short story collection, *Theetu.* He has published one novel, *Thagappan Kodi*, three short story collections and two poetry collections, *Nee Nikalthana Podhu* and *Arubha Nanju.* His collection of essays is titled, *Vetkam Ketta Nadu.* He has received several awards for his writings, including the Best Writer award from the Tamil Nadu Government in 2003.

Vizhi Pa Idhayavendhan

Vizhi Pa Idhayavendhan is the pen name of P Annadurai. A prolific Dalit writer, he has over twenty-two books to his credit, including stories, poetry and plays. His writings have appeared in journals including *India Today* and *Dinamani Kadir*. His stories have been featured in Tamil, as well as in translation into English and Malayalam, in Sahitya Akademi publications. He has won several literary awards, and students have researched his writings for their M.Phil and Ph.D. Degrees.

ABOUT THE TRANSLATORS

Malini Seshadri is a freelance writer, editor and translator with several years of experience in all these areas. She has translated several Tamil works into English for publication, including one dalit novel and several short stories. She has authored/co-authored several books including school text books on science and values education.

Ramakrishnan is an Engineer-turned-literature-graduate pursuing his Ph.D. in English at the University of Madras. Equally fluent in English and Tamil, he indulges in creative writing and translation in both languages. This is his first published work of translation.